CYBER STORM

ISBN: 978-1-7369881-5-2
LCCN: 2021922504

This publication is designed to provide accurate and authoritative information with regard to the subject matter covered. It is sold with the understanding that the publisher is not engaged in rendering legal, accounting, or other professional advice. If legal advice or other expert assistance is required, the services of a competent professional should be sought. The opinions expressed by the authors in this book are not endorsed by TechnologyPress™ and are the sole responsibility of the author rendering the opinion.

Most TechnologyPress™ titles are available at special quantity discounts for bulk purchases for sales promotions, premiums, fundraising, and educational use. Special versions or book excerpts can also be created to fit specific needs.

For more information, please write:

TechnologyPress™
3415 W. Lake Mary Blvd. #950370
Lake Mary, FL 32746
or call 1.877.261.4930

CYBER STORM

TechnologyPress™
Lake Mary, Florida

CONTENTS

CHAPTER 1

CYBERCRIME THROUGH THE YEARS

BY GREGORY MARRON
President and Owner – The Marron Group, Inc.

Since the dawn of time, criminals have been taking advantage of others in order to benefit themselves. Every type of community is susceptible to criminal behavior, and as our society becomes more dependent on the Internet, we also become more vulnerable to cybercrime. These criminals cost companies in the United States over half a billion dollars annually. But how did we get here? Let's take a look at the origin of cybercrime and how cybercrime has grown to affect our daily lives.

Cybercrimes are criminal offenses committed on the Internet or aided by the use of technology where computers or networks are a tool, target, or the place of the criminal act. The first known act dates back to 1834, when a couple of robbers attacked a network by hacking the French telegram system. They stole information from the stock market, essentially carrying out the world's first cyber-attack.

However, "cybercrime" is a term that has only become popular in the past 20 years. Before the prefix "cyber" became ubiquitous, criminals did not need a computer to commit fraud, traffic child pornography, steal intellectual property or identity, or violate someone's privacy. All those activities existed before "cybercrime" became a well-known term or criminal practice. Cybercrime represents an extension of existing criminal behavior alongside some novel, illegal activities. Hackers were once seen as bringing power to the little guy – the only opposition to large corporations and monopolies. Now people mostly view hackers as enemies of society.

Hundreds of years ago, maritime trade traveled through the same circular networks we have now, and pirates continually tried to hack those networks. For trade to take place, there must be a network that allows goods to be exchanged. Piracy can't exist without successful trade being there first, which is why in the 15th through 18th centuries, pirates followed the trade networks like a trail of breadcrumbs to steal riches from their victims. They were hacking a trade network just like those who try to get illegal access to something online today. At one point in history, pirates moved textiles, sugar, and slaves, holding them for ransom. Similarly, today hackers will lock down a personal computer or, for example, an electrical grid for ransom money.

As technology and networks have evolved, so have the acts of piracy. For example, two years after Alexander Graham Bell invented the telephone in 1878, the Bell Telephone Company had to remove a group of young boys from the telephone grid in New York for repeatedly and purposely misdirecting and disconnecting customer calls.

Phone network hacking became popular in the 1950s, when a group of "phreaks" (a term that was coined in 1972), short for phone freaks, hijacked portions of the world's telephone networks, making unauthorized long-distance calls and setting up special "party lines" for fellow phreaks.

Next, the proliferation of computer bulletin board systems (BBSs) in the late 1970s provided an environment where the informal phreaking culture began to coalesce into quasi-organized groups of individuals who graduated from the telephone network to hacking corporate and government computer network systems.

More recently, the rise of social media and the tendency of its users to pack their profiles with detailed personal information provide bad actors key intelligence to carry out cybercrimes.

Cybercrime ranges across a spectrum of attacks. Some involve breaches of personal or corporate privacy and identity theft. Others are transaction-based crimes like fraud, digital piracy, and counterfeiting, which involve specific crimes with specific victims. Another aspect of transaction-based crimes involves individuals within corporations or government bureaucracies deliberately altering data for either profit or political objectives. In contrast, other types of cybercrime often disrupt the functionality of the Internet. These others range from spam, hacking and denial-of-service attacks against specific sites to acts of cyberterrorism – which involve the use of the Internet to cause public disturbances and even death. For example, in 2015, Ukraine's electrical grid was hacked in the middle of winter. The grid's physical infrastructure was overloaded by cyberterrorists, causing it to shut down. This meant people lost electricity and heat during extremely cold weather, resulting in deaths for some who were exposed to the elements.

Here are examples of the most common and damaging types of cybercrime:

- *Business e-mail compromise (BEC)* scams exploit the fact that so many of us rely on e-mail to conduct business – both personal and professional. It's one of the most financially damaging online crimes.
- *Identity theft* happens when someone steals your personal information, like your social security number, and uses it to commit theft or fraud.
- *Ransomware* is a type of malicious software or malware that prevents you from accessing your computer files, systems, or networks and demands you pay a ransom for their return.

- *Spoofing and phishing* are schemes aimed at tricking you into providing sensitive information to scammers.
- *Online predators* are a growing threat to young people.

As we grow more dependent on the Internet for business and personal use, our chance of becoming a victim of cybercrime increases. In the last five years, the FBI IC3 (Internet Crime Complaint Center) has received 2,211,396 complaints about cybercrime, with $4.2 billion in losses.

In 2020, the cybercrime that had the highest victim count in the United States, with 241,342 cases, was "phishing/vishing/smishing/pharming." Victims of these crimes receive unsolicited e-mails, text messages, and telephone calls purportedly from a legitimate company requesting personal, financial, and/or login credentials.

Business e-mail compromise (BEC) and e-mail account compromise (EAC) affected the most people in 2020, totaling $1.8 billion in financial losses. BEC is a scam targeting businesses (not individuals) working with foreign suppliers and/or businesses that regularly perform wire transfer payments. EAC is a similar scam that strictly targets individuals.

These sophisticated scams are executed by bad actors who compromise e-mail accounts through social engineering or intrusion techniques to conduct unauthorized transfers of funds. They target people based on their objectives. People over the age of 60 represent the largest age group of victims.

The year 2020 will forever be synonymous with the Covid-19 pandemic. Fraudsters saw this as an opportunity to exploit the pandemic by targeting both businesses and individuals. That year, the IC3 received nearly 29,000 complaints related to Covid-19. Fraudsters went after the Coronavirus Aid, Relief, and Economic Security Act (CARES Act), which included provisions to help small businesses during the pandemic.

A Timeline Of Cybercrime:

1957 – Joybubbles: Joe Engressia (Joybubbles), a blind seven-year-old boy with perfect pitch, heard a high-pitched tone on a phone line. He began whistling along to it at a frequency of 2,600 Hz. This enabled him to communicate with phone lines, thereby becoming the US's first phone hacker or "phone phreak" (to use the terminology first used in 1972).

1971 – Steve Wozniak and Steve Jobs: After Steve Wozniak read an article about Joybubbles and other phone phreaks, he became acquainted with John "Captain Crunch" Draper and learned how to hack into phone systems, using a blue box he built for the purpose. He used this power by pretending to be Henry Kissinger and prank-calling the Pope. He started mass-producing the device with friend Steve Jobs and selling them to classmates.

1981 – First cybercrime conviction: Ian Murphy, aka "Captain Zap," hacked into the AT&T network and changed the internal clock to charge off-hour rates at peak times. The inspiration for the movie *Sneakers*, he's the first person convicted of a cybercrime. Murphy was sentenced to perform 1,000 hours of community service and serve two and a half years of probation.

1988 – The Morris Worm: Robert Morris released something on the Internet many consider to be the first worm. To show that the author was a student there, the worm was released from a computer at MIT.

1995 – The first hacker Kevin Mitnick made the FBI's Most Wanted list: Kevin Mitnick penetrated some of the most heavily guarded networks in the world, including Nokia and Motorola. He leveraged specialized social engineering systems, tricking insiders into handing over codes and passwords and used codes to breach internal operating systems.

1999 – The Melissa Virus: A virus-infected Microsoft Word records, automatically transmitting itself via e-mail as an attachment. It was mailed out to the first 50 names mentioned in the Outlook e-mail address box of an infected device.

2017 – WannaCry: WannaCry, the first known example of ransomware operating via a worm (viral software that replicates and distributes itself), targeted a vulnerability in older versions of Windows OS. Within days, tens of thousands of businesses and organizations across 150 countries were locked out of their own systems by WannaCry's encryption. The attackers demanded $300 per computer to unlock the code.

2017 – Equifax: Equifax, one of the biggest US credit bureaus, was compromised, revealing 143 million customer accounts. Social security numbers, birth dates, addresses, driver's license numbers, and certain credit card numbers are part of the confidential leaked information.

2021 – Colonial Pipeline hack: An analysis of the cyber-attack on the Colonial Pipeline found that the hackers were able to access the company's network using a compromised VPN password, Bloomberg reported. The hack led to a ransomware payout of $4.4 million and resulted in gas prices around $3 per gallon for the first time in several years at US gas stations.

WHAT IS THE MOTIVE BEHIND CYBERCRIME?

As in the past, financially motivated attacks continue to be the most common. About 96% of all attacks are financially motivated, followed by espionage, grudge, and fun. Likewise, bad actors categorized as organized crime continue to be the #1 perpetrators of cybercrime.

While the motive for cybercrime is overwhelmingly financial, targets of cybercrime vary from individual property to organizations, governments, and wanting to attack society at large. Cyber security is the good guys' response to cybercrime. It is the art of protecting networks, devices, and data from unauthorized access or criminal use. It's also the practice of ensuring confidentiality, integrity, and availability of information. Taking the right security measures and being alert when connected are crucial to preventing cyber-intrusions and online crimes.

Since most of the world is now connected by the Internet, that makes cybercrime a global threat. In response, numerous countries have developed cybercrime laws to go after criminals. Cybercrime legislation can be tracked by the first-ever Global Cyberlaw Tracker, developed by the United Nations Conference on Trade and Development (UNCTAD). It tracks the state of e-commerce legislation in four fields:

1. E-transactions
2. Consumer protection
3. Data protection/privacy
4. Cybercrime adoption in the 194 UNCTAD member countries

The tracker indicates whether or not a given country has adopted legislation or has a draft law pending adoption. In some instances where information about a country's legislation adoption was not readily available, "no data" is indicated.

Cybercrime laws have been adopted globally in the following areas and to the extent represented below by its 194 UNCTAD member states:

- 82% countries with e-transactions laws
- 80% countries with cybercrime laws

- 66% countries with privacy laws
- 56% countries with consumer protection laws

The Internet has provided the world a vast network of connectivity to work, communicate, and exchange commerce. But history often repeats itself, and much like pirates of the 15th century who attacked and looted successful trade networks, today's hackers and fraudsters see the Internet as a treasure trove of endless possibilities. Piracy has progressed and evolved since the 15th century, so it's undeniable that cybercrime is escalating and growing in complexity alongside our global trade networks.

As this threat escalates and cybercrime starts hitting closer and closer to home, it's important that we know there is no such thing as "perfect security." If someone can build a wall, there's always someone trying to knock it down. The best things you can do to make yourself less vulnerable are to keep your operating system up-to-date, install and keep antivirus software current on your computer and be cautious of downloading questionable files. You wouldn't leave the doors and windows of your home open and unlocked, so don't do it with your computer.

About Gregory

Gregory Marron is the president and owner of The Marron Group, Inc. where he leads a team of technical engineers who have a combined 120 years of experience. For the past two decades, Gregory has worked in the technology industry for companies where he was in charge of network security for offices here in the US and around the world. His career has included working for an international publisher, a software developer, a wholesale food distributor, and a leading international law firm, including distribution and promotions management. He has often been charged with the implementation and management of network architecture for voice, data, and security, which has required him to stay current on the installation of and support for the latest technology.

Gregory felt drawn to the IT industry through a desire to help in a field that is in great need of assistance. Cyber security is growing exponentially, and because of that, skilled workers are in high demand. His curiosity also influenced his career path. He wanted to investigate cyber security threats and attacks to find out why certain events had occurred and how to prevent them from happening or doing damage in the future.

Gregory loves the fact that working in cyber security means no two days are the same. New threats are a constant in this industry – a challenge he gladly accepts. Over the years, he has relied on skills like problem-solving, technical aptitude, and fundamental computer forensics, but his desire to keep learning has been instrumental in his success. Gregory is driven by the challenges that accompany an ever-evolving industry like cyber security that constantly presents new threats and technologies.

The Marron Group, based in the Chicagoland area, specializes in providing hands-on technology, architecture solutions through installation, support, and management of a company's technology footprint. The Marron Group provides IT services for small to mid-sized businesses. They also focus on ensuring that each client's technology is properly aligned with its strategic goals. Their services include:
- Management of IT services
- Cyber security
- Remote workforce
- VoIP services

In addition to leading The Marron Group, Gregory also does *pro bono* work for a global nonprofit organization whose goal is to provide positive guidance for individuals and families. Gregory also provides thought leadership for future technology advancements.

You can connect with Gregory at:
- Web: https://www.TheMarronGroup.com
- E-mail: Greg@TheMarronGroup.com

CHAPTER 2

WHY EMPLOYEE EDUCATION IS YOUR FIRST LINE OF DEFENSE

BY DAVID SPIGELMAN
Owner and CEO – Working Nets

Imagine – you upgrade your home security system, and this time you pay a whole lot of money to get all the bells and whistles. You have confidence in the equipment and the provider's services, so you feel like your house and family are safer than ever. Then, one day, your 12-year-old son Jackson rushes out of the house, gripping a skateboard in one hand, biting into an apple with the other. His buddy Matty is skating in the street, doing tricks. Jackson hops on his board, and they roll out of the cul-de-sac. Sunlight shines through the open door as if pointing to the brand-new game console. A teenage boy walks by and notices. He sees no cars in the driveway and no movement inside. He effortlessly enters and unplugs all the electronics he can carry, then sneaks into the master bedroom and sweeps jewelry off the dresser and into his coat pockets. He darts between the houses and is never seen again.

How the heck could this have happened? It's simple. You, the parent, didn't take sufficient steps to ensure the technology would be effective. You forgot the human component of safety measures.

You didn't teach everyone in the family who is capable of turning a knob *why* it's important to close the doors or how to set the alarm. The robbery is not entirely Jackson's fault. Although it seems like common sense to close a door when leaving the house, he felt more connected to the feeling of the wheels hitting the concrete than protecting possessions.

Too many businesses make this same mistake and skip educating the team about cyber security. Your company may invest large amounts of money and time procuring technological tools that protect environments from cyber threats, but it will be all for naught if your people aren't included in the process. Even the most sophisticated systems will be ineffective if you don't cultivate a culture that emphasizes security as part of the paradigm. It is essential to commit to ongoing training – and that includes imparting a shift in mindset.

HOW TO CREATE A SECURITY-MINDED PARADIGM

Executives, you can't simply have management teach a few lessons on e-mail threats and expect significant progress toward safety-oriented behavior. You need to think bigger. Your goal is to adjust the tint of the lens through which employees perceive their responsibilities, so they will always approach tasks through a security-minded filter.

In terms of behaviors to enforce, you'll need to regularly evaluate and adjust the approach to consider any changes in context or setting. For example, if you hold open the door for a stranger carrying a stack of pizzas, have you done a good thing? Maybe. It depends on the social paradigm. On the other hand, would you let in a person who is chasing someone into the building and wielding a knife? Clearly, opening the door for a runner with a weapon is a hard "No!"

When I worked as a government contractor, the agency's security paradigm was instilled in us and influenced the way we thought and acted. A keycard and code were required to enter the building, and we respected this because we valued the objective – to protect citizens' private records. Since we understood the reason people without proper authorization were not *supposed* to get in, it was easy to push aside our socially conditioned manners and follow the rule to not let anyone at all into the building.

An ancillary benefit of embedding security into the company's cultural paradigm is that it can relieve the pressures of decision-making when conflicted by social norms. In this type of environment, if you behave in ways that might otherwise be considered rude, coworkers will not look askance. And the safety-oriented mindset will decrease the likelihood that employees will engage in unsafe behaviors. This will alleviate the need to bother with disciplinary-related tasks, such as lifting up keyboards to check for passwords written on sticky notes.

EVERY SINGLE PERSON IN THE ORGANIZATION IS A RISK

An attacker only needs a single action from one employee – one click, one download – to access the network. Once inside, they can steal money and data, then demand exorbitant ransoms, all of which seriously damage a company's reputation. A seemingly small mistake can destroy your entire organization.

And it's not only your *company's* data that's at risk. Consider that many companies have special access to their strategic partners' network environments via virtual private network (VPN) connections. Although encrypted, if your information systems are compromised, the attackers also have an entry to your partners' data. In fact, some attackers target small companies only because they provide a backdoor to reach these partners.

Entering a system from the outside is challenging, but lucky for cybercriminals, they know that hacking an individual is an easy way to slip into the network. They are often shrewd scholars of human flaws. For one, let's face it – people are fundamentally lazy.

Our intolerance for inconvenience has worked out pretty well for us as a species in some ways. Our desire to find an easier, faster, more efficient way of doing things has led to vast technological advancements. The tendency to look for the quickest options backfires, though, when it comes to security. Hackers know to direct their attacks at the soft underbelly of the company – its people. And the employees are especially attractive targets since they have a higher clearance level than outsiders.

Staff truly pose the biggest cyber-security danger to an organization, so it is critical that *everyone* at all tiers of the company is trained in security procedures. You'll need to implement a top-down initiative, meaning C-level executives agree that they will not give themselves a pass on compliance. If *anyone* is perceived as exempt from following security protocol, inevitably, others will not take the policies seriously either.

FOSTER A CULTURE IN WHICH EMPLOYEES CARE ABOUT THOSE YOU SERVE

Another way to change the paradigm is to make sure employees are invested in the mission of your work and that they value those you serve. Think of a reputable physician's office where the staff's entire purpose is to provide patients with the best possible care. If the whole team is taught to understand that protecting a patient's privacy is just as important as their health, the culture alone may be enough to ensure they properly guard personal health information (PHI).

Medical staff and agencies are considered "covered entities" under the Health Insurance Portability and Accountability Act of 1996 regulations, which was designed to protect PHI. However, HIPAA is only effective if everyone understands – and cares about – the rules. Anyone who has access to the data needs to recognize that it is very personal and can be sensitive. For example, Mr. Johnson probably doesn't want the entire waiting room to hear that his anti-schizophrenia meds are ready. It might embarrass him. He may also fear that he'll be treated differently – or even that it could cost him his job. Laws that apply to any industry can help enforce actions but are ineffective without the human component.[1]

ESSENTIAL TRAINING

Here are some basic policies and procedures to teach employees in any organization. Keep in mind that this is by no means an exhaustive list.

1. Credential Policies

a. *Passwords:* Years ago, the National Institute of Standards and Technology (NIST) came up with the notion that the epitome of credential security was a password composed of eight characters that included uppercase, lowercase, numeric and typographical symbols. There was little if any, data to support this idea, but the entire industry bought into it.

We have the data now, though, and found out that a password like *5(2sKuYq* is very difficult for humans to remember, which is why so many people write them down. Not only are these scribbled passwords easy for others to find, but they are also a cinch for computers to crack.

New studies tell us that a passphrase with all lowercase letters, such as *brainycashewtarget*, is actually much more computationally secure and far easier to remember. And the current NIST recommendations are to remove

---

1. U.S. Department of Health & Human Services (2020, December 10), The HIPAA Privacy Rule, https://www.hhs.gov/hipaa/for-professionals/privacy/index.html

periodic password change requirements altogether.

This is a safe practice when you use a passphrase following these guidelines:

- Include 15 or more characters.
- Make it memorable, so you don't have to write it down.
- Make it unusual, so humans and computers are unable to figure it out.

A phrase like *dunkingdonutsinlimeade* is 22 characters. Once you imagine the visual, it's hard to forget. However, it would be very difficult for humans to guess. It is also a much more computationally challenging method than the earlier requirements and could take thousands of years to brute-force.[2]

b. *Password sharing:* In short, don't do it. There is generally no reason that anyone needs someone else's password. If Franklyn is out of the country, and it is absolutely critical that Jackie retrieve a file that's available only on his computer, first, we must question why he's the only one with access to it. Second, Jackie does not need his password to open the document. If it is an emergency, an administrator should be able to access the computer, even if it's by changing Franklyn's password.

c. *Credential responsibility:* Put a policy in place to hold users responsible for actions taken using their credentials. If the logs show that user Tasha deleted a file, then Tasha is at fault for having deleted it, even if she did not take this action herself. The threat of real consequences may prevent Tasha from leaving her

---

2. National Institute of Standards and Technology, US Department of Commerce (2021, August 30), NIST Special Publication 800-63B Digital Identity Guidelines: Privacy Requirements (4.4), https://pages.nist.gov/800-63-3/sp800-63b.html#memsecret

computer unlocked while she steps away or sharing her password with a coworker.

d. *Multi-factor authentication:* MFA is a process that uses an external system to authenticate credentials. It offers an important layer of security and should be set up and enforced if available. Microsoft and Google both have such authenticator apps for use on your smartphone. Once it's set up, login attempts trigger a request sent to the app for approval or issue a prompt to enter the number provided by the app for the given system. Either way, MFA helps protect against unknown third-party access.[3]

2. E-mail Security

E-mail is one of the most common attack vectors today because it is delivered directly to every user's computer and mobile devices.

a. *When it comes to security, trust your instincts!* Humans are very good at detecting when something doesn't seem right. It's a function of our fight-or-flight system that lives in the old part of our brain. Unfortunately, the neocortex – the newer, more rational portion of the brain – likes everything to be okay and often squashes our danger radar. When it wins, we pretend things are normal, even if we sense that something's wrong. *Pay attention to your gut feeling!*

If any part of an e-mail seems strange, it is worth taking a longer look. Watch out for odd or vague wording – e.g., "I can't believe you in picture Saturday. http://...?" Be suspicious. Is the sender someone who e-mails you regularly? Pick up the phone and call to verify that they actually sent you that message. And if the domain

---

3. Mary Shacklett (2021, May), "What Is Multi-factor Authentication?" TechTarget, https://searchsecurity.techtarget.com/definition/multifactor-au thentication-MFA

doesn't match up to the known URL (e.g., "Microsoft Support" <sally@somedomain.notmicrosoft.br>), *delete it immediately!*

On the other hand, many dangerous messages can also be carefully crafted, with only subtle clues that something is wrong. One client received an e-mail from what appeared to be a vendor requesting a wire transfer payment of $60K. Although this was not a standard payment method for the business, it seemed plausible because it included a copy of a recent invoice. It looked like it could have been real, but upon closer examination, the domain was slightly off (e.g., "digitil" instead of "digital"). If someone asks for money in a way not previously agreed upon, *call before sending the payment.*

b. *Use caution when clicking links.* In many e-mail systems, if you hover your mouse over a link, you will see the full URL. Get into the habit of checking to confirm that the URL matches the expected website address before clicking on it. Also, be aware that cybercriminals often mimic legitimate websites with mock-ups. Download links are *very dangerous* and can lead you to inadvertently open the network's front gates and invite attackers in directly through your computer.

3. Company-wide security training

Consider hiring an outside training company or working with your third-party trusted IT services firm. No matter your IT team's or provider's level of competence, they are not likely skilled trainers. It's worth investing in professionals who are versed in communicating with employees to effect change.

CONCLUSION

As employers, remember that we can increase the chances that employees – as well as ourselves – will do the right thing by making sure every single person understands their role's importance in the success or failure of the company. Executives have a particular responsibility to model secure practices to protect data. I cannot stress this enough. Everyone is significant – and anyone, from intern to CEO, has the ability to open a door to cybercriminals.

Once you create a culture with a paradigm that includes everyone in security practices, the behaviors can fall into place. A paradigm that can protect your company from cyber-attacks is also possibly the most important key to building a thriving organization.

Sources

1. U.S. Department of Health & Human Services (2020, December 10), The HIPAA Privacy Rule, https://www.hhs.gov/hipaa/for-professionals/privacy/index.html
2. National Institute of Standards and Technology, US Department of Commerce (2021, August 30), NIST Special Publication 800-63B Digital Identity Guidelines: Privacy Requirements (4.4), https://pages.nist.gov/800-63-3/ sp800-63b.html#memsecret
3. Mary Shacklett (2021, May), "What Is Multi-factor Authentication?" *TechTarget*, https://searchsecurity.techtarget.com/definition/multifactor-authentication-MFA

About David

David Spigelman is the Owner and CEO of the IT company, Working Nets. A teacher at heart, David is passionate about security awareness education. And like most IT firms, his Baltimore-based company, Working Nets, provides services based on the scientific principles of technology, but an appreciation for organizational psychology and the user experience sets them apart.

Always looking to find better ways to improve, David worked with a "Why Coach," whose practice is based on Simon Sinek's *Start With Why and Finding Your Why*. He learned that his WHY – the inspiration for his approach to business and life in general – is "to create clarity."

David believes it is important for people to understand how systems function and why particular changes are necessary, whether they're technical or behavioral. This is because knowing the purpose behind a studied method is key to compliance and investment. He applies this philosophy when serving smaller companies with outsourced network support and says it helps to elevate their game and fortify their place in the "bigger playgrounds."

He likes having the opportunity to make an impact on organizations that don't have the resources to employ full-time IT and network engineering staff. Working with small businesses allows Working Nets to have a direct connection with decision-makers instead of spending time navigating layers of management and bureaucracy.

Although the company does not take on larger organizations as clients, they provided David with invaluable experience as an employee. He worked as the network administrator at the American Center for Physics and ran the network security team at Amerix Corp. He also built and prepared firewalls for local Social Security Administration centers to enable state SSA offices access into the federal system.

David has a degree in electronic engineering and technology from the ITT Technical Institute in Carson, California. He was born in Los Angeles and has lived in Baltimore for 27 years, but eventually would like to make Jerusalem his home.

He is married, with five children and eight grandchildren. David and his wife, Stacy, are wellness coaches after having lost a combined 135 pounds, which they have kept off since 2012. Following that drive to teach others, they have helped hundreds of people realize long-term health by adopting better habits.

On another personal note, he loves to sing and even has perfect pitch! One day, he'd like to learn to play an instrument.

And here's one of David's favorite quotes: "We imagine a world in which the vast majority of people wake up every day inspired, feel safe wherever they are and end the day fulfilled by the work they do." – Simon Sinek

Contact Working Nets:
- Twitter: @workingnets
- Web: https://workingnets.com
- Phone: 443-992-7394

CHAPTER 3

WHAT IS RANSOMWARE AND HOW TO AVOID PAYING MASSIVE RANSOMS

BY SUNIL RAINA
Owner & President – TeamLogic IT

Ransomware: All Over The News – And All Over The Internet
According to the US Department of Justice Technical Guidance
document *Protecting Your Networks From Ransomware*,
"Ransomware is the fastest growing malware threat, targeting
users of all types – from the home user to the multinational
corporate network. On average, more than 4,000 ransomware
attacks have occurred daily since January 1, 2016."[1]

In recent times, ransomware attacks and computer security
breaches have set off a parade of blaring headlines and breaking
news stories. *In the face of such relentless coverage, people may
be tempted to tune out the subject entirely. Even those whose
businesses are at risk from ransomware can be overwhelmed in
the face of this very threatening and rapidly spreading problem.*

---

1. US Department of Justice Technical Guidance document: Protecting
   Your Networks From Ransomware https://www.justice.gov/criminal-ccips/
   file/872771/download

THE PROBLEM IS HUGE AND GROWING

How many attacks are happening today? An accurate estimate is elusive because many victims of ransomware would rather pay quietly and return to business than face the bad publicity and loss of public trust that disclosure might bring. Still, the ransomware tidal wave continues:

- A Cloudwards survey reports that 51% of respondents were hit by ransomware attacks in 2020, with the average small business subjected to demands of $5,900.[2]
- A Comparitech report on ransomware attacks on the health care sector estimates that in 2020 some 92 attacks, affecting more than 600 hospitals and clinics, cost nearly $21 billion.[3]

RANSOMWARE IN THE HEADLINES – AND IN THE SOFTWARE UPDATE NETWORKS

Two ransomware attacks in the first half of 2021 garnered incessant media attention. The shutdown of the Colonial Pipeline company interrupted the movement of fuel along a 5,000-mile distribution network. Panic hoarding led to short-term shortages of gas and diesel. The company paid a ransom of $5 million in cryptocurrency, although a portion of this was recaptured by law enforcement.

The attack on the IT services company Kaseya had consequences for its MSP customers worldwide, as well as for downstream customers: the shutdown of a grocery chain in Sweden and the disruption of New Zealand schools. Altogether about 60 companies were severely affected, with lesser effects for as many as 1,500 companies using Kaseya's VSA software update services. The hackers demanded $70 million in ransom.

---

2. Cloudwards.net report: *Ransomware Statistics, Trends and Facts for 2021 and Beyond* https://www.cloudwards.net/ransomware-statistics/
3. Comparitech.com report: *Ransomware Attacks On US healthcare Organizations Cost $20.8bn In 2020* https://www.comparitech.com/blog/information-security/ransomware-attacks-hospitals-data/

NOT ALL ATTACKS MAKE BIG HEADLINES

In May 2019, the hacker group RobbinHood seized partial control of the online infrastructure of Baltimore, Maryland. They demanded ransom in Bitcoin amounting to some $76,280. The city council, police department, public works, finance, recreation and parks, archives and records, housing, and zoning appeals, were all impaired to varying extents. City services, from building permits to parking fines to court scheduling systems, had to conduct business by paper, pen, and telephone. The city refused to pay the ransom, and it took more than a month – and an estimated $18 million – to restore its systems to normal function.

In August 2019, the IT systems of 22 small Texas towns were "hacked, seized and held for ransom in a widespread, coordinated cyber-attack" that set emergency-management officials scrambling. Media accounts don't name the towns, and the various agencies and government departments involved were tight-lipped, saying that only portions of the computer systems were affected and blaming the attack on "one single threat actor." [4]

HOW MANY ATTACKS ARE LIKELY IN 2021 AND BEYOND?

Sobering statistics from the security firm Safe At Last:

- In 2021, ransomware attacks against businesses are expected to occur every 11 seconds.
- One in 3,000 e-mails that pass through filters carries malware.
- Large organizations pay an average ransom of $233,217 to regain control of their data and systems.
- The average downtime following a ransomware attack is 19 days.

---

4. Manny Fernandez, Mihir Zaveri and Emily S. Rueb, "Ransomware Attack Hits 22 Texas Towns, Authorities Say," *The New York Times*, August 20, 2019, https://www.nytimes.com/2019/08/20/us/texas-ransomware.html

Predictions are speculative in this rapidly evolving environment, but Safe At Last suggests that costs associated with ransomware attacks and recovery will likely far exceed $20 billion in 2021 and could rise to as high as $5 trillion by 2025.

A BRIEF HISTORY OF RANSOMWARE

The earliest acknowledged ransomware attack occurred in 1989. Malware was spread via 20,000 floppy disks containing a Trojan horse virus, which were distributed to attendees at a WHO conference on AIDS. The malware was set to awaken the 90th time an infected machine was booted up. The AIDS Trojan hid directories and encrypted the names of all files on the users' C\: drives. A pop-up message demanded payment.

The rise of the Internet enabled the widespread distribution of malware and also provided hackers an expanding field of potential targets. Ransom attacks accelerated dramatically with the advent of cryptocurrencies, which made possible large, untraceable transactions.

WHAT IS RANSOMWARE?

Most ransomware attacks originate from malware inserted into a system. When activated, the malware encrypts files and holds the system hostage until a ransom is paid. If the demand is denied, the attacker could unleash malware that destroys all files on the system. Some hackers add on blackmail, threatening to expose trade secrets or corporate misdeeds. Ransomware can block access to your system (or block your customers from accessing theirs), disable databases, and sabotage accounting and banking systems.

HOW DO HACKERS GET RANSOMWARE INTO MY NETWORK?

Ransomware is often delivered through exploit kits such as

watering-hole attacks. These can include counterfeit versions of websites frequently used by staff members of a company. The phony pages are crafted to look familiar but include links that download malware or forms that fraudulently collect information. Other delivery methods include malicious advertising and e-mail phishing campaigns that include disguised links or attached files that trigger malware downloads. All these are designed to fool inattentive or unsuspecting individuals into entering sensitive information or downloading malware.

HOW ARE SYSTEMS CORRUPTED?

"One of the common mistakes people make with a ransomware attack is they come in in the morning, they see their data has been encrypted, and they think the attack happened that night," says Peter Mackenzie, incident response manager for the security firm Sophos, in a video interview with Mathew Schwartz of the site: GovInfoSecurity. When the crypto-locking malware announces itself, attackers have typically been inside the network for days, weeks, or months. Mackenzie says attackers "often deploy the ransomware overnight when fewer admins are watching, but the actual attack is normally days or weeks longer than that." Sadly, says Mackenzie, not many enterprises have the skills or the staff to continuously patrol their systems for infiltrated malware.[5]

HOW TO DEFEND AGAINST AN ATTACK

A robust, up-to-date security program is vital. If this seems a burden from the perspective of budgeting or staff training time, remember this: *Like a parachute, it's much better to have a ransomware defense plan and not need it than to need it and not have it.*

---

5. Matthew Schwartz, *Government Info Security*, June 26, 2021, https:// www.govinfosecurity.com/ransomware-strategies-for-faster-detection-response-a-16902

TECHNICAL DEFENSES FOR SYSTEMS AND SOFTWARE

In a fast-evolving multiverse of cloud computing, remote work, VPNs, and bring-your-own-PCs, it is crucial to build and maintain a multifaceted defense against the vulnerabilities of IT systems. You'll need to create and deploy a pre-incident preparedness strategy that includes backup, asset management, and restriction of user privileges. Other benchmark standards for effective defense:

- Design and implement a robust program of endpoint protection that can work on advanced algorithms, running in the background 24/7.
- Set up frequent, regular backups. Intermittent or weekend-only backups risk the loss of a week or more of work product.
- Locate copies of backups on separate devices in different locations.
- Regularly check to make sure your backups can be retrieved.
- Maintain a comprehensive patch and update protocol to protect systems from known and unknown vulnerabilities.
- Segment your network to guard against the proliferation of malware throughout your system.
- Deploy advanced anti-phishing protection.

CREATE A CULTURE OF SECURITY AWARENESS

Every bit as important as system defense is the need to cultivate a culture of security awareness and preparedness in your most important asset – the humans who operate your business. People are both the weakest link and the first line of defense in protecting the integrity of your IT systems. To effectively avoid and defend against breaches, accidental or malicious, you must instill a security-first mindset, beginning with training that equips staff to quickly detect, avoid and report potential threats.

Four Keys To Effective Security Awareness Training

1. *Create interactive education and training programs* – A culture of awareness is not a one-and-done task. Engage staff from top to bottom by working with them one-to-one regularly, with lots of time for dialogue.
2. *Require commitment, instill accountability* – Give the staff tools and clear instructions, solicit formal commitment to using them and reward exemplary practices.
3. *Eliminate ambiguity* – Identify specific risky actions, such as using unvetted flash drives or insecure file transfer sites and provide precise instructions for avoiding those dangers.
4. *Make training continual and vary techniques* – Conduct educational sessions several times a year and add interim measures, such as newsletters, supplemental training videos, threat alerts, and security checks.

SHORT-TERM OUTLOOK

As the 2020s began, cyber security experts noted a trend away from scattershot phishing campaigns (known as "spray and pray") toward targeted attacks on bigger enterprises, termed "Big Game Hunting." For example, the July 2021 Kaseya attack directly affected some 60 IT service providers, and the downstream damage extended to hundreds of schools, retailers, dental practices, and CPA firms worldwide. The perpetrators demanded a ransom of $70 million to cover all the affected systems.

"...now even wannabe hackers who lack high-level technical skills can launch ransom attacks..."

This does not mean smaller companies face any less risk of attack. Ransomware as a service (RaaS) is an emerging business model in which developers lease ransomware components the same way legitimate SaaS developers lease theirs. Some dark web RaaS services offer support, user forums, and other features of legitimate SaaS models. This means that now even wannabe hackers who lack high-level technical skills can launch ransom attacks for profit.

The immediate solution is to join forces with a managed security services provider with a proven record of success in preventing or stopping ransomware attacks.

IS ZERO TRUST THE NEXT LINE OF DEFENSE?

Unlike the traditional firewall standard for protecting IT systems, this approach assumes that no visitor can be trusted, challenging every network access request. Nowadays, a person could be working from an enterprise network, a coffee shop, home, or anywhere else in the world. The resources they access may be spread across many systems, whether on-premise or in multiple cloud environments. Regardless of the visitor's location or prior login, Zero Trust security always responds with, "You have zero trust with me! I must thoroughly verify you before granting access to any resource." The baseline is "Never trust, always verify." Zero Trust is inconvenient – even frustrating – for users, but it may well prevent an expensive breach.

LONG-TERM OUTLOOK

With hyper-focused media attention and new US and international government cyber security responses, we may witness some evolution in the tactics of ransomware perpetrators.

One recent development is that more companies buy insurance to pay the ransom and other costs of attacks. *The perpetrators are seemingly a step ahead – there are reports of ransom hackers searching a potential victim's network for details on their insurance and matching their ransom demands to the limits of the policy.* This may be only another skirmish in the escalating war between legitimate business systems and their unscrupulous attackers.

WHAT'S A BUSINESS TO DO?

Understandably, the owners and managers of small to medium-sized businesses are too busy doing business to build and maintain a full-time defense against an ever-evolving ransomware threat. By now, people reading this know it too: you need to partner with a well-known and trusted security service provider who can design and maintain an "active defense" regime. The best of these can document consistent investments in technology, as well as form partnerships with trusted cyber security organizations in both the private and government sectors.

When choosing a security-focused MSP, look for one that offers deep resources and an ongoing commitment to stay ahead of the "bad guys."

Sources

1. US Department of Justice Technical Guidance document: *Protecting Your Networks From Ransomware* https://www.justice.gov/criminal-ccips/file/872771/download
2. Cloudwards.net report: *Ransomware Statistics, Trends and Facts for 2021 and Beyond* https://www.cloudwards.net/ransomware-statistics/
3. Comparitech.com report: *Ransomware Attacks On US healthcare Organizations Cost $20.8bn In 2020* https://www.comparitech.com/blog/information-security/ransomware-attacks-hospitals-data/
4. Manny Fernandez, Mihir Zaveri, and Emily S. Rueb, "Ransomware Attack Hits 22 Texas Towns, Authorities Say," *The New York Times*, August 20, 2019, https://www.nytimes.com/2019/08/20/us/texas-ransomware.html
5. Matthew Schwartz, *Government Info Security*, June 26, 2021, https://www.govinfosecurity.com/ransomware-strategies-for-faster-detection-response-a-16902

About Sunil

Sunil Raina is the President of TeamLogic IT of Ellicott City and BWI. This MSP, based near Baltimore, Maryland, offers a team of industry experts in IT consulting, cyber security, and network support, combining many decades of experience serving small and medium-sized business customers. Under Sunil's leadership, TeamLogic IT provides unmatched excellence in service delivery and responsiveness to small and medium-sized businesses.

Sunil earned a BSc in physics, chemistry, and mathematics from the University of Kashmir, India, and an MBA in finance and international marketing from the University of Baltimore. He has also completed the Executive Program at the Wharton School on Leading The Effective Sales Force.

Prior to opening TeamLogic IT of Ellicott City and BWI, Sunil held executive sales and global business development positions with several multinational corporations in Europe and the US. His experience spans industries including telecommunications, life science technology, and quantum electronics. This wide corporate background affords him the experience and insight to quickly grasp the unique challenges of IT clients of all sizes and industries, while keeping the focus on end-user satisfaction and service delivery excellence.

At TeamLogic IT, Sunil and his highly accomplished team of IT professionals help businesses fortify their networks using customized IT and cyber security solutions. IT services include proactive cyber security protection, cloud computing, backup and disaster recovery, business continuity, mobility, IT procurement, and consulting services. His company also provides domain expertise for compliance with CMMC, NIST 800-171, HIPAA, FINRA, and other industry standards.

Whether a customer needs IT outsourcing in its entirety or supplemental to their own internal IT activities, TeamLogic IT offers customized solutions to meet both requirements. As part of a nationwide network of more than 230 offices, TeamLogic IT can scale its services to work with practically any size enterprise, all across the US. Driven by industry best practices, penetrating research into evolving industry trends, and a skilled, deeply committed staff of technicians and engineers, TeamLogic IT was also ranked the 2020 First Place MSP Of The Year winner in the Channel Futures MSP 501.

Sunil brings rich insight and perspective to everyday life from his extensive travels around the world. He calls Maryland home, having resided there with his wife and two sons for more than 20 years. He is a keen reader with strong interests in IT, technology, international affairs, travel, yoga, and social causes. In his free time, he loves to run, spend time with the family and watch the Discovery Channel.

Contact Information:
- E-mail: sraina@TeamLogicIT.com
- LinkedIn: https://www.linkedin.com/in/sunilraina/
- Twitter: https://twitter.com/Cyber_IT_Xperts
- Facebook: https://www.facebook.com/TeamLogic-IT-1252417304823628
- Web: https://www.teamlogicit.com/ellicottcitymd006/
- Phone: 443-574-7280

CHAPTER 4

BACKING UP YOUR DATA

BY BOB SAVAGE
CEO and Founder – Savage Consulting, Inc.

Back in 1999, when I was first starting out as an IT professional, I joined an organization called Network Professionals. They provided trade leads to smaller businesses like mine. One night, a dental office was having a problem, and they couldn't get in touch with their regular IT guy. Because they were in a pinch, I was pulled in.

I was able to fix everything for them straight away, and they ended up keeping me on as their new IT guy. I remember thinking that the whole environment was so interesting: X-ray machines and patient records. It all felt so official, and the work I was doing was directly helping others. I was sort of hooked.

From that point on, I tailored my marketing toward dental offices throughout the Tampa and St. Petersburg area of Florida. My business went from a one-man show to a functioning team that services dental offices from Vero Beach up to Gainesville.

In the last 20 years, I've watched as the industry began embracing digital X-rays and saw how incorporating them changed their practice for the better. Now I'm helping build systems that can handle 3D imaging. Everything we do is customized, and everything is monitored and inspected remotely from our location with both online and phone-based IT services.

One of the biggest things businesses should focus on is data backup, or – more importantly – business continuity and disaster recovery.

Many business owners believe that if they just keep copies of their data saved on external hard drives, they're covered. While that's certainly better than doing nothing in terms of data backup, it's an antiquated and often risky practice to rely on. For the last five to ten years, the best practice has been to save things to the cloud. This way, your information is saved online and can be accessed remotely if needed.

Data backup is often overlooked or, at best, handled as cheaply as possible. This is partly because, when people think about taking extra efforts to back up their data, they are generally only thinking about how to keep their files safe in case a computer crashes. While that's certainly important, an underlying aspect to data backup often goes unnoticed: keeping that data *secure* and preventing hackers from getting into it.

HOW THIS PERTAINS TO RANSOMWARE

Hackers have evolved as quickly as technology has, and one of the trending terms in cyber security today is "ransomware." There are a number of ways ransomware can get into your computer without you noticing, and when it does, it can be a nightmare for your business or personal life.

Predatory e-mails are among the most common methods hackers use to infiltrate your computer system. They are especially difficult to detect because they could resemble a thousand completely normal e-mails you see on a day-to-day basis. Many of them share the first and last name of someone you might be familiar with or could include a link to an article about the latest technology in your industry. Whatever the link *says* it is, in the case of ransomware, it's poison for your security system.

Malware will download onto your computer, encrypting everything you have on the server with an encryption key that only the hacker knows. That hacker will then hold your data, along with the data of your clients and staff, for ransom in exchange for that encryption key. Unless you pay at that point, you won't be able to access anything or even use your computers.

In the entire time I've been in business, I've only had one partner who had to pay the ransom. In this case, he didn't listen to my advice regarding proper data backup. Ransomware infected his server, and the business was down for a week while we unencrypted the server. We had no choice but to pay the ransom to get the encryption key.

Because that partner paid the ransom once, the hackers took note. Two months later, they struck again. This time, however, we'd backed everything up properly and taken precautions. We were up and running in a couple of hours. Once the ransom is paid, the hackers know that your data is valuable and you are willing to pay, and this makes you a prime target.

With our Business Continuity and Disaster Recovery (BVDR) service, your data is inspected for signs of ransomware when it is uploaded to the cloud at night. We've had situations where we were told about the ransomware the following morning and were able to delete the malicious files and links before they started the encryption process. However, if the encryption had started, we restore it to the hour before the ransomware was received. At that point, the joke is on the hacker.

HOW DATA GETS LOST

There are five main ways businesses can lose their data:

1. *Human Error:* Accidental deletion/changes to data continue to be a key driver for data loss. Sometimes you'll edit a file, save it as the wrong name and then overwrite another important file and you've lost it, or you can delete something you don't mean to delete. "Drag and drop," while certainly convenient, only makes it easier to delete things by accident. Accidental deletions impact productivity because workers may have to spend time repeating previous work to recreate documents. In a doctor's office, this could include important X-ray scans, important health information updates, or billing information.

2. *Ransomware attacks, malware, and data corruption:* Data can be lost or damaged due to malicious cyber-attacks.

3. *Hardware failure:* Despite improving hardware reliability, laptops still last on average three years, making data loss due to sudden hardware failure a reality.

4. *Hardware can also be physically stolen:* I had a client whose tower server was physically stolen from his office. If it's all backed up to the cloud, it's no big deal: we can just set you up on a virtual server while we build you a new server. You won't lose anything. Statistically, break-ins happen at night, so your stuff will be completely backed up from the day before. As the workforce becomes more mobile, it is more likely devices such as laptops will be lost or stolen.

5. *Data can be lost because of environmental events:* Whether it's to protect against fire, hurricane, or tornado damage, you need to put safeguards in place for your data. Where we live, hurricanes are the chief concern. I remember one time a hurricane came through, and a business we serviced disconnected all their IT equipment and placed it in the

basement to protect it without labeling any of it. We then had to put everything back to where it belonged but had no idea where it came from. Had they been using our BCDR service, they wouldn't have had to worry about moving their equipment and losing data.

COSTS OF DATA LOSS

At the very tip of the iceberg, we have the obvious: data loss means downtime.

This means a loss of sales or, for a doctor, this could be a lack of patients you can work on. It also means a loss of employee productivity, missed deadlines, an inability to communicate with clients or patients, lost e-mail, an inability to bill clients, the cost to restore IT systems, and ultimately, client dissatisfaction.

Client dissatisfaction is perhaps the most detrimental of the consequences because if clients can't get what they need from you for long enough, they are going to go somewhere else. This could impact your bottom line and your business's reputation tremendously.

Then there are the legal ramifications. In the event of ransomware and a breach of 500 or more records, dental and medical offices are required to report the breach to the Office for Civil Rights, which will then perform a HIPAA audit. If any discrepancies are found during that audit, you will be fined. These fines run between $150K and $250K for a typical six-doctor office.

In addition, you would have to send a letter to each patient informing them of the breach. By law, you would then have to offer those patients identity insurance for 12 months following the breach. These patients could also file lawsuits, further damaging your business's reputation and financial stability.

If you take appropriate measures to prevent a data breach, you could avoid these costly repercussions. By being able to stop things like ransomware in their tracks, you will protect your patients and could ultimately save your business.

WHAT CAN BE DONE

In order to truly tackle this problem, business owners should adopt an intensive, thorough approach.

When we first started out, I used mirrored hard drives on my computer. They did the job well enough at the time, until one day both hard drives failed simultaneously.

Now, with BCDR, we are able to take a snapshot of your server every hour, and then, at the end of the night, it uploads all of that to the cloud. This limits the risk of data loss substantially. If your system crashes at 4:00 p.m., you'll have everything up to 3:00 p.m. saved.

I also have a technician check to make sure all our partners' servers are backed up every day. If not, we are on the phone with you and will monitor your server remotely to make sure we get it working quickly.

By using BCDR, we are able to virtualize you within hours, so you can operate off an online server while you wait to have yours fixed and rebooted. It runs only slightly slower than what you're used to, and it can be the difference between a couple of hundred dollars and thousands while we conduct a restore.

I had a partner recently whose server went down during a holiday at about 3:00 a.m. We virtualized everything and even found some ransomware. If he'd saved his stuff the old way, that ransomware would have gone undetected, and it could have cost him everything. Because he listened to us, we were able to virtualize him for 30 days, and his business carried on without a hitch. They didn't lose any money, they didn't have to pay a fine, and they didn't lose business to their competitors.

When put up against the cheaper option – merely using an online backup that just uploads your files and folders to the cloud once a night – there is no comparison. Business Continuity and Disaster Recovery is a little more expensive up-front, but it's worth it in the long run.

It means billing insurance companies on time, detecting problems before they get out of hand, avoiding fines and legal trouble, and not having to wait weeks to have everything recovered and fixed.

BCDR is something every business should consider. Many offices think they can't afford it, but if your server were to fail or receive ransomware and your office wasn't able to work for a week, how much revenue would be lost while your server was being rebuilt or repaired?

Most offices we service would lose close to $100K a week.

Think of proper data backup as a form of insurance. It protects your customers and patients while saving you time and money in the long run. Ultimately, proper data backup could save your entire business, allowing you to focus on what really matters: providing the best, most secure service to your clients and partners.

About Bob

Bob Savage is the CEO and founder of Savage Consulting, Inc. What began initially as a simple newspaper ad for IT work has grown substantially over the last 20 years. Today, Savage Consulting, Inc. provides specialized IT services to dental offices throughout the Tampa and St. Petersburg area of southwest Florida.

Before founding Savage Consulting, Bob worked as a radar technician in the army. While serving, his military specialization focused on fixing mobile radar units while they were onsite. Insatiably curious, Bob spent his years after the service in a variety of vocations that ranged from testing B-52 bombers to finding out what might happen to electronics in case of a nuclear attack, to building houses, working as an auto mechanic, and even owning and driving 18-wheeler trucks across the country.

While he was driving professionally, Bob found himself called back to his true passion: working in technology. At the time, a friend of his decided to start a pet supply business. He brought Bob in to set up computers for the company and help out whenever. It was here that he realized how much he enjoyed working in IT. After gaining experience running IT for the pet supply business, he launched Savage Consulting, Inc. Eager to learn everything he could, he returned to school and went on to receive certifications in A+, Network +, Security+, and three additional Microsoft Certified Engineer certificates.

One of the most important facets of his approach as an IT professional is to focus on the people he's working with, saying, "At any point in my life, when business was down and I focused on the numbers, my business only suffered more. When I started to not worry about all of that and focused on the people, my business always improved. It's about establishing and maintaining good relationships with good people...always."

Bob believes the secret to success in business is to surround yourself with people who can teach you something new or can further expand your expertise. Adamant about keeping ahead of the curve, he has taken business courses and hired business coaches to ensure he's consistently developing his skills as a CEO to adapt to an ever-changing climate. His most recent endeavor has involved a 52-week leadership course.

When he's not focusing on his continued education, Bob enjoys cycling, flying, target shooting, and spending time with his wife, Ellen.

You can reach Bob at:
- Email: Bob@SavageConsulting.net
- LinkedIn: Savageco
- Web: https://savageconsulting.net
- Phone: 813.240.7772

CHAPTER 5

SECURING YOUR DATA IN THE CLOUD

BY JOHN STOCK
Founder, Owner and CTO – DymaTech, Inc.

In this age of virtual resources, businesses have more options than ever for economic and flexible data storage and management. For most small to medium-sized businesses (SMBs), cloud storage is a great way to use their limited resources wisely while still retaining all the functionality and room for quick growth that they need.

However, as a professional in the IT support industry, I have come across a lot of people who have said they wanted to move their company data to the cloud because they think that will magically help them with security. They often believe that data stored in the cloud automatically ensures that the data is more secure and that this is ensured by whatever cloud provider they are using.

Unfortunately, what these people don't realize is that there is no homegrown, built-in security for a server in the cloud. Unless you implement security on the server you set up in the cloud, it will remain unsecured, and essentially you would have just put up a free server on the web for anyone to access. This creates a whole world of issues for which you are now legally liable. It is imperative for everyone, especially business owners, to understand that while moving and storing data in the cloud can be extremely helpful and practical, it does not instantly solve security concerns. There is work to be done to make the cloud a secure place for your data. Data stored in the cloud must be secured, and there must be a plan in place for the preparation, moving, storage, and upkeep moving forward after the move.

It is important to note that this is often a common misunderstanding, even among professionals who would be considered "tech-savvy." One group of developers working on some custom software had their database servers up on the cloud. They assumed the cloud server was providing security, although they had not set any up themselves. Their Amazon Web Services (AWS) overages were pretty consistent from month to month – suddenly, they received a bill for $40,000 for one month's use, even though their usage had not changed. They soon discovered that someone had accessed their unsecured server and was using their resources to mine Bitcoin.

Since there was no security set up (even though the developers thought there was security built into the server), this is not considered a "hack" because there was not technically anything to break into. This is an important legal distinction for liability. So, when the developers filed a claim with their cyber insurance for the $40,000, the claim was denied immediately. The insurance provider cited a clause in the policy (one every cyber insurance policy has) that the policy only provides coverage on the condition that full security measures are taken and compliance regulations are met. Cyber insurance, while very necessary, does not cover negligence and lack of due diligence. If you have your data in the cloud, you need to validate to the right people that you are doing everything possible to secure it.

This is a particularly crucial point for SMBs that are operating with limited resources. Many SMBs are using legacy software or older hardware. Making the move to storing their data in the cloud is a great economical choice for these businesses with outdated equipment. It is cheaper to rent hardware and cloud storage for monthly fees than to spend tens of thousands of dollars on new hardware that needs to be maintained, housed, powered, etc.

The best way to make sure your data is secure, no matter where it lives, is to partner with a third-party IT security firm. Not only will they implement the correct security measures to bring your company up to compliance, but they will also perform continual monitoring, tests, and updates, so you are constantly protected in a field of rapidly changing crime. Just as with on-site infrastructure, cloud systems need continual maintenance and updating. Many providers will offer to include patch management with their products, but they may not offer regular vulnerability scanning or application patch management. Vulnerability scans can uncover open ports, unpatched applications, or new vulnerabilities of any other kind.

Here is a list of steps that are crucial to securing your data in the cloud:

1. *Put up firewalls and security monitoring.* Just like you would put them on your physical storage devices, you need firewalls and security monitoring on your virtual storage. This is important to have on both ends – in your cloud server and on the devices accessing it. Additionally, your cloud security should be tested, just as your devices are.

2. *Use comprehensive encryption.* Most cloud providers use volume-level encryption. This type of encryption works well for physical media loss and provides definite advantages even in cloud environments but adding file-level encryption gives your data an additional layer of security.

3. *Confirm your cloud provider's security.* Although they are not responsible for the security of your data on your cloud servers, your cloud provider must have security policies that exceed your own. Make sure they are fully compliant with

any regulations you must adhere to, and those that require third-party audits and certification. Ask for evidence of their compliance and audits before trusting your sensitive data to them. In addition, your cloud provider can give you documented confirmation that your data is completely isolated from any other client data. This documentation is important to have so you can prove that your provider has claimed responsibility for this isolation. This may sound like a lot, but keep in mind that your contracted security advisor firm will handle this document management for you.

4. *Create backups of all your data.* Another common misconception around storing data in the cloud is that since most cloud providers co-locate data for redundancy, you do not need to back up your data. I spoke with a client recently who said his cloud provider synchronized his data to multiple locations so that if a location went down, his data could be brought online at another data center. I asked if he had considered what would happen during a malware attack on his data, and he responded that the provider could just bring his data up on another site, as with any other outage. I pointed out that if the synchronization was real-time, as the provider said it was, all the sites would be infected as well. The client went silent. It was obvious that this very real possibility had not been discussed or prepared for. This is an area in which SMBs will often try to shortcut to keep costs down, but as with any other part of security, there are no shortcuts that do not end in a breach. Backups can be in another cloud server or on physical devices, but they are essential.

5. *Have a recovery plan.* In the event of a catastrophic data loss, there must be a plan for data recovery. Make sure you have a documented disaster recovery and business continuity plan that considers your recovery point and recovery time goals. This plan should also be broken into specific protocols by data categories. It should include which data is most important

(rankings), how long your business can tolerate data loss from the different categories, how quickly you need each type of data restored, etc. This is another resource best built with your security advisor, who can become familiar with your business processes and systems and make informed decisions about what your recovery plan needs to look like. In many high-transaction environments, productivity losses are calculated by the minute. Always remember that just because your data is in someone else's data center, it does not mean you can trust it to their recovery practices. Your business must have its own.

6. *Organize and categorize your company's data.* This allows you to know and document what type of data is stored in each location, which in turn means you can set up access procedures, so it is always handled appropriately based on its sensitivity. An added advantage is that you can prioritize setting the tightest security measures around the most sensitive data, which means you will be using your security resources and attention efficiently. All of this will help gain and maintain compliance and mitigate liability.

7. *Adopt the zero-trust security model.* The zero-trust security model could (and does) occupy a book of its own. In short, zero-trust security is the concept of an organization not trusting anything outside or inside their network – instead, the organization always assumes a breach is being attempted and requires verification before granting access. It entails implementing controlled access policies, least privileged access models, verifying devices and applications, etc. This model has become even more important as cloud-based infrastructures and working from home are becoming more commonplace. A successful implementation of the zero-trust model is complex and must only be attempted with a professional.

Short of true zero-trust implementation, controlled access

is a basic necessity for cyber security. Some of the basic policies for this are:

a. Enforce strict password policies. Some guidelines now recommend entire phrases rather than just words. For an added layer of security, multifactor authentication is an important way to put the brakes on an attacker. Even if you fall for a phishing attack, multifactor tools or an approval process will alert you that someone is attempting to sign in. Hackers can create additional access methods once they are on a system that still works after the user has changed their username and password, so the key point is to do everything possible to prevent that initial access.

b. Set up end-user device security. Everyone who is granted access to your network must have fully compliant security enabled on every device used. You can have the best cloud security possible, but if a user with weak end-point security can access your data, so can others. Make sure end-user data access is limited to only the data required to perform their functions (e.g., employees can access what is needed for their jobs but no more). This is another instance in which data categorization is highly useful. If a user needs temporary access to sensitive data, make sure their access will expire automatically, either after a specified period of time or after a predetermined number of connections.

c. Use secure data transfer. Encrypted tunnels, such as VPNs, provide an important layer of security when your data is in motion.

d. Have a plan for employee separation. This process is to keep track of everything a user can access and ensure that the access is disabled as soon as that user is no longer a part of the organization. Especially in the case of a disgruntled former employee, there must be a mechanism in place for locking them out of all systems quickly.

8. *Provide ongoing annual security awareness training with HR.* There are many options for providing this, both in-person and online, and this is another area in which your security contractor can advise you. Whether you choose to implement lengthy, structured training or short, frequent trainings, find one that is effective and can be tested periodically with simulations to measure the effectiveness and identify users who may need additional support.

It is important to remember that no matter how much security is implemented, there is always the potential for pitfalls and breaches. Technology advances to improve business, but the same technologies can be used by others to destroy businesses. The perimeter of your business is no longer the boundaries of your network or physical space. The new perimeter is global, and it must be approached from a global point of view. This is the best way to keep the barbarians outside the gates and prepare for when the gates are breached.

About John

John Stock is the chief technology officer of DymaTech, Inc., a company he founded in 2016. John has worked with information systems since the early '90s, though he was introduced to technology engineering much earlier. As a child, John watched his father work as an aerospace engineer. On special days, he was allowed to go to work with his father and watch the team work on groundbreaking projects. This engineering influence followed him as he started writing basic programs when he was still very young. In college, he pursued a degree in engineering and took many business classes as well. After college, he began work as a branch manager and eventually became a regional financial controller while gaining certifications and continuing his IT education. During a period of expansion through acquisition, his company established a formal IT department, and he was promoted to director of information services. He was responsible for establishing a central data center and converting the array of systems onto a common platform. Through this, he helped the company grow from one small office to 60 throughout North America. He has been in corporate IT ever since.

From the beginning, his passion for technology was rooted in problem-solving, as well as an empathy for those coming to him with problems. His time as a financial controller and business manager kept the business perspective of IT in view. He learned early on that the goal is not just to ensure the technology is working – it is to make sure people can get their work done efficiently and live their lives.

Over the years as an IT professional, he outsourced to many IT companies and was struck by the lack of urgency and understanding for their clients' businesses. The attitude seemed to be that the client could wait and be fine, as long as it was not a major outage. He felt strongly that any IT issue could impact the business – what may seem like a minor inconvenience could mean a company is unable to meet a deadline and an employee is unable to get to their kid's game, all because a technology issue wasn't treated with urgency and understanding. He knew it was time to provide a solution and start a company that would see the business and the people, not just the technology. He promised himself his company's differentiator would be that they would understand people's business and their priorities and remain empathetic to the fact that anything could have an impact on a client's business and personal lives. Now, as cyber security is the latest arena where things are changing rapidly and it is crucial to keep up, John and his company are meeting the new challenge.

DymaTech is located in Newport Beach, California, and specializes in providing tailored IT services for small and medium-sized businesses. Like their founder, they are people-oriented problem-solvers.

You can reach John at:
- E-mail: sales@DymaTech.com
- LinkedIn: https://www.linkedin.com/company/dymatech-inc
- Web: https://DymaTech.com

CHAPTER 6

WHY EVERY C-SUITE EXECUTIVE HAS A DUTY TO PREPARE FOR A CYBER-ATTACK

BY STEPHEN CRACKNELL
CEO & Owner – USM Technology

Great things are done by a series of small things brought together.
~ Vincent van Gogh

The most dangerous attitude a C-suite executive can have about cyber security is thinking a cyber-attack could never happen to their organization, so there's no reason to implement a recovery plan. Some executives say they aren't concerned because their assets are too small to pique a hacker's interest. Tell this to the senior citizens tricked out of a couple hundred bucks after their e-mail accounts are hit.

Others may think that they are safe because they already spend plenty on cybersecurity. Well, leadership at Apple, Chase, and even some branches of the federal government know firsthand that their financial resources do not make them invincible. The truth is that there's no silver-bullet technology to guarantee cybercriminals will not infiltrate a network. If it existed, these behemoths would have been the first in line to purchase it. Instead, they joined the ranks of countless other cybercrime victims spanning the past decade.[1,2,3]

We cannot afford to underestimate the capabilities of today's cybercriminals. Hackers are ruthless, calculated, and organized. They have demonstrated an utter lack of compassion for humanity by stealing from our grandparents, and they have proven high levels of competence by figuring out how to break into the largest, most well-funded organizations on earth.

So, here is the uncomfortable question you must consider. If your organization invests less money and time in cybersecurity than the large entities that have been hacked and are a richer target than the average elder, is there any legitimate reason to believe hackers won't eventually breach your network too and demand a ransom?

WE ARE FIGHTING A WAR

The moniker "cyberwarfare" is no exaggeration, considering war is "a state of competition, conflict or hostility between different people or groups." US-based organizations are the targets of organized cybercrime syndicates that regularly consolidate under hostile nations to steal money from us – so, by definition, this is a war. (lexico.com, 2021)

To emphasize the severity, here are two sobering facts about the cybercrime industry:

- The global cost of cybercrime has climbed from $3 trillion

1. Kartikay Mehrotra (2021, April 21), "Apple Targeted In $50 Million Ransomware Hack Of Supplier Quanta," *Bloomberg,* https://www.bloomberg.com/news/articles/2021-04-21/apple-targeted-in-50-million-ransomware-hack-of-supplier-quanta
2. James Coker (2021, August 23), "US State Department Hit By Cyber-Attack," *Infosecurity Magazine,* https://www.infosecurity-magazine.com/news/us-state-department-cyber-attack/
3. Ravie Lakshmanan, Ravie (2021, January 10), "Russian Hacker Gets 12-Years Prison For Massive JP Morgan Chase Hack," *The Hacker News,* https://thehackernews.com/2021/01/russian-hacker-gets-12-years-prison-for.html

in 2015 to $6 trillion in 2021 and is expected to reach $10.5 trillion by 2025.[4]

- The head of the US National Security Agency stated, "Cybercrime constitutes the greatest transfer of wealth in human history."[5]

The business of cybercrime continues to grow, in part because, although the US federal government knows who many of the key actors are, they are unable to prosecute the most nefarious groups. This is because these criminals are protected by nations that financially benefit from the attacks. Immunity allows attackers to safely develop increasingly sophisticated strategies that lead to escalated levels of damage and more frequent hits. And the greater harm hackers inflict, the higher the ransom they can demand to halt the destruction. As profitability grows, these groups reinvest and the cycle continues, each time more successful than the last.[6]

PREPARE FOR THE WORST

If your organization has repelled a minor cyber-attack in the past, don't be lulled into a false sense of security – surviving a mosquito bite in a land where hungry lions run free does not make you unsusceptible to a big cat attack. Be prepared to respond to the worst-case scenario. It's easier to scale back recovery efforts than amp them up during a crisis.

Beware of an extremely harmful and common tactic called the *human-operated ransomware attack*. The actors often start with

4. Steve Morgan (2020, November 13), "Special Report: Cyberwarfare In The C-Suite: Cybercrime To Cost The World $10.5 Trillion Annually By 2025," *Cybercrime Magazine*, https://cybersecurityventures.com/hackerpocalypse-cybercrime-report-2016/
5. Josh Rogin (2012, July 9), "NSA Chief: Cybercrime Constitutes The 'Greatest Transfer Of Wealth In History,'" *FP Insider*, https://foreignpolicy.com/2012/07/09/nsa-chief-cybercrime-constitutes-the-greatest-transfer-of-wealth-in-history
6. William Dixon (2019, February 19), "Fighting Cybercrime – What happens To The Law When The Law Cannot Be Enforced?" *World Economic Forum*, https://www.weforum.org/agenda/2019/02/fighting-cybercrime-what-happens- to-the-law-when-the-law-cannot-be-enforced/

classic hacking techniques to enter the target network. In teams, they conduct reconnaissance, exfiltrate data, and elevate their network privilege and access. This prep work prior to launching the actual attack enables exponentially more damage than with other types of cyber-attacks.

Here's a walk-through of what could happen to you: Hackers research your organization through publicly available information to learn about your business model, profitability, and pressure points. They find out everything they can about your leaders and their habits. They then enter the network – possibly through targeted phishing. Once inside, they conduct the kind of research that can only take place *within* your network. They attempt to move laterally while escalating their access privileges. They also make a concerted effort to leave themselves multiple "backdoor" entrances to more easily return if the first attack fails. They attempt to exfiltrate sensitive data and house it on their servers for use as future blackmail fodder. Since they are about to have great success converting your organization into a paying client, they can't wait to return! And that won't be the last time.

HACKERS ENTER QUIETLY AND LEAVE NO TRACE

How do they get away with this? Sophisticated hackers wait until your organization is most vulnerable – off-hours when leadership is disconnected from technology or a time when your industry is typically preoccupied. They know that an accounting firm is most vulnerable in the middle of tax season, and a retail chain is an easy hit during the Christmas rush. Executives, hackers are watching you. They follow your CEO's family on social media, so when their spouse posts details of an upcoming overseas vacation, they can plan an attack for these dates.

To kick off the strike, hackers trigger a self-propagating virus to disable recovery tools, destroy backup files and prepare your network for the attack. Then they launch the ransomware, which crawls across the network and encrypts any sensitive data files it can access.

The final step, like Boy Scouts departing a campsite, is to make sure they *leave no trace*. They clean up the crime scene, making a concerted effort to eliminate all recorded evidence of their activity. This process includes deleting log files, which makes your recovery efforts all the more challenging since your forensics team relies on the log files to answer these important questions: Which techniques did the actors use to penetrate the network? When did hackers first infiltrate the network? Which systems and users were compromised? Hackers know that without this information, your recovery effort will be prolonged and likely incomplete, so they will have an easier time re-entering your network.

To ensure you are able to answer those questions, continuously route critical log files to a secure off-site system capable of dynamic analysis. This populates a repository for the forensics team to review in the aftermath of an attack. This system can also alert your technical team when suspicious activity is occurring inside your network, so you'll be better poised to stop an attack from escalating.

UNITED WE PLAN

A house divided against itself cannot stand.
~ Abraham Lincoln

Your best defense is a united front and a well-executed plan. During a major cyber-attack, the entire executive team must operate as a cohesive unit and share one common goal. Leadership's mantra should be "We shall restore our core business processes as quickly as possible."

It is incumbent upon business leaders to work with their IT team to build out a robust incident response plan and to do so immediately. If you do not have one in place, your group will be forced to build it *after* the attack is launched, likely at two in the morning. At this point, staff will be exhausted and likely locked out of the tools they need to document your path to recovery, and meanwhile, the ransom clock continues to tick.

If the executive team participates in the document creation and approval process, then the leaders will have the time and resources needed to set post-attack priorities. These priorities will help to guide the rapid recovery of the organization's critical business processes during a crisis. The fewer questions and details to sort out during the crisis, the faster your cyber-response team can act and the more likely they will operate as a cohesive unit in the first critical days after a cyber-attack. Moving forward quickly gives your group a better chance of finding an alternative to paying the ransom.

Conversely, if your organization responds to a cyber-attack with internal disputes and focuses on assigning blame, you create a hacker's dream dynamic. After launching an attack, their primary objective is to divide the people who are responsible for recovery efforts. They want to make your technical executives look foolish and incompetent because when the team loses faith in them, the organization as a whole will become feeble and ineffectual. Cybercriminals have learned that they are typically well-positioned to receive a ransom payment in the near future when a leadership team spends most of its energy fighting against itself.

A SOLID INCIDENT RESPONSE PLAN FOR THE WIN

By failing to prepare, you are preparing to fail.
~ Benjamin Franklin

When disaster strikes your organization, a well-designed incident response plan becomes the difference between surviving an attack and becoming yet another victim. This plan should include a list of team members who will participate in the recovery effort, a workflow of activities, vital network configurations, and contact details for employees and vendors as well as key clients. Everyone should know in advance which tasks they are responsible for completing and have the necessary resources at the ready.

It's critical for your company to have a plan in place to quickly spin up a clean "recovery network" for secure communications. E-mail and phone systems may be compromised during the attack, making it difficult to coordinate recovery efforts. You may need to wait days or even weeks before these platforms can be fully reestablished on the infected network.

Be prepared for hackers to taunt the leadership team, saying how easy it was to break into your network while providing very clear instructions for how to pay the ransom. They want to convince you that making the payment is the only way to restore your network, and they work to make the ransom transaction effortless. They are getting very, very good at it, by the way. Some cybercriminal syndicates will even offer a "support desk" to set up a cryptocurrency account and expedite payments.[7]

THE FIRST 72 HOURS ARE CRITICAL

Your recovery team's ability to work effectively in the first three days after a ransomware attack is essential to successfully rebuff the cybercriminals. We recommend your goal be to have your core business processes back online within 72 hours of the attack to minimize the loss of income and productivity and to avoid paying the ransom.

Expedience is everything. You won't have time to debate when to call in the insurance company or which cyber-recovery consultants to hire. Your IT team cannot wait for Finance to

---

7. James Crawley (2021, July 19), "Anatomy Of Ransomware Attack: Chat Support, A Discount And A Surcharge For Bitcoin. CoinDesk, https://www. coindesk.com/markets/2021/07/19/anatomy-of-ransomware-attack-chat-support-a-discount-and-a-surcharge-for-bitcoin/

approve spending requests or for the COO to decide which systems should come back online first.

This time frame is key because hackers often put limits on how long they will wait for payment. They know that as each hour passes, the likelihood that they will get paid drops precipitously. As a result, they often implement fallacious deadlines to add pressure. At the 72-hour mark, they may threaten to double the ransom or, after seven days, refuse to sell you the decryption key.

Don't give priority to less important issues, such as the hunt for culpability, determining how the hackers infiltrated your network, assessing damage, or responding to inquiries by outside entities. These other efforts can happen alongside recovery efforts but are secondary. Throughout the initial critical days, regularly remind yourself and your team that none of these competing objectives will matter if your organization goes bankrupt as a result of not resuming core business processes in a timely manner.

Recovery from a major attack will take many days or weeks, so everyone must be ready to deal with the inevitable exhaustion. Make sure your response teams work in shifts and that your staff and leadership are given time to recuperate. If you do not plan for this, fatigue will cause focusing difficulties, poor memory, otherwise avoidable mistakes, and irritability.

Also, know that paying the ransom is not a "Get-Out-Of-Jail-Free" card. The hackers may demand more money after you pay the initial amount. They may accept your money but not send you the key or send one that only works to unlock certain files. Once your organization has paid a ransom, chances dramatically increase that the hackers will use one of the back doors they left open to return, re-encrypt your files and start the whole process all over again. Or they may threaten to release sensitive information that they exfiltrated to the media, competitors, or your clients. And there is no avoiding the ugly truth that some of the ransom you paid will fund their next round of attacks.

THREE ESSENTIAL RESOURCES NEEDED TO RECOVER A NETWORK

Whether working with an external IT firm or your internal department, after a cyber-attack you'll need to give the technical professionals access to these vital tools in order to recover your network:

1) *Off-site Data Recovery Solution:* A ransomware-resilient off-network data recovery solution will allow critical servers and their data to be quickly brought back online after an attack.

2) *Off-site Log Repository:* A comprehensive off-site Security Incident and Event Management (SIEM) solution that gathers, analyzes, and stores key log files will allow a forensics team to determine how and when the hacker first entered a network.

3) *Incident Response Plan:* Key details about critical business processes, network configurations, and a plan for the initial response, along with contact information for key vendors, clients, and staff, poises you for a successful recovery.

CYBERCRIME IS A SERIOUS MATTER

Globally, malicious cybercrime continues to escalate in severity and frequency. As a business leader, you have a duty to ensure your organization is prepared for battle. You need to have a robust incident response plan in place so, in the event of a cyber-attack, you and the other C-suite executives are in a position to model efficacy, inspire unity, and quickly recover those core business systems.

ARE YOU READY TO TAKE ACTION?

During a serious cyber-attack, your incident response plan becomes your company's most valuable asset. To help your C-suite executives start this critical recovery planning process, we have developed a resource that outlines the core components. (https://guide.usmtechnology.com)

Sources

1. Kartikay Mehrotra (2021, April 21), "Apple Targeted In $50 Million Ransomware Hack Of Supplier Quanta," *Bloomberg*, https://www.bloomberg.com/news/articles/2021-04-21/apple-targeted-in-50-million-ransomware-hack-of-supplier-quanta

2. James Coker (2021, August 23), "US State Department Hit By Cyber-Attack," *Infosecurity Magazine*, https://www.infosecurity-magazine.com/news/us-state-department-cyber-attack/

3. Ravie Lakshmanan, Ravie (2021, January 10), "Russian Hacker Gets 12-Years Prison For Massive JP Morgan Chase Hack," *The Hacker News*, https://thehackernews.com/2021/01/russian-hacker-gets-12-years-prison-for.html

4. Steve Morgan (2020, November 13), "Special Report: Cyberwarfare In The C-Suite: Cybercrime To Cost The World $10.5 Trillion Annually By 2025," *Cybercrime Magazine*, https://cybersecurityventures.com/hackerpocalypse-cybercrime-report-2016/

5. Josh Rogin (2012, July 9), "NSA Chief: Cybercrime Constitutes The 'Greatest Transfer Of Wealth In History,'" *FP Insider*, https://foreignpolicy.com/2012/07/09/nsa-chief-cybercrime-constitutes-the-greatest-transfer-of-wealth-in-history

6. William Dixon (2019, February 19), "Fighting Cybercrime – What happens To The Law When The Law Cannot Be Enforced?" *World Economic Forum*, https://www.weforum.org/agenda/2019/02/fighting-cybercrime-what-happens-to-the-law-when-the-law-cannot-be-enforced/

7. James Crawley (2021, July 19), "Anatomy Of Ransomware Attack: Chat Support, A Discount And A Surcharge For Bitcoin. *CoinDesk*, https://www.coindesk.com/markets/2021/07/19/anatomy-of-ransomware-attack-chat-support-a-discount-and-a-surcharge-for-bitcoin/

About Stephen

Stephen Cracknell is the CEO and Owner of USM Technology. He founded Dallas and Houston based USM Technology in 2010 to provide IT solutions and cyber security services to mid-market organizations across the US. Along with his wife, Stephen also owns US Medical IT, a managed services provider (MSP) that caters to the health care industry.

USM Technology assists businesses with IT projects, cloud computing environments, servers, networking, and help desks. Their highest priority, though, is to help business leaders repel cyberattacks.

He has witnessed the destructive power of ransomware firsthand too many times. In one case, cybercriminals dismantled a healthy business – a small medical clinic – in a matter of minutes. After the attack, the physician-owner reached out for help. It turned out that ransomware had encrypted the medical records server as well as the backup drives that were connected to the network. Unfortunately, the doctor didn't know he needed to maintain an offline copy of the backup files. If he had received the right training and preparation, the clinic would still be operating today. On the flip side, the team at USM is energized when helping IT leaders implement technology such as custom automation, digital forms, workflows, and business intelligence to evolve their business and enable staff to reach their potential.

Stephen knows about the creative use of ones and zeroes himself. During his 12-year career at Microsoft, he worked on many projects involving security, databases, and network architecture. Then, after Hurricane Katrina hit the Gulf Coast, he was asked to assemble a team to design a digital registration system for American Red Cross disaster shelters. Stephen's team formulated a ruggedized, battery-powered solution that allowed volunteers to digitally collect and relay demographic and medical details of displaced persons – even when the disaster area lacked power and Internet. Bill Gates was so impressed that he presented Stephen and his team with Microsoft's Innovation Award. Stephen built on these experiences when he launched USM Technology. The company has been a Microsoft Gold Competency Partner for over a decade and was twice named Microsoft's South Central US Partner of the Year.

Stephen holds a bachelor's degree in economics and finance from the University of Guelph in Ontario, Canada. He currently serves in a leadership role with the Health Industry Council Foundation of North Texas and is a member of Voices for Innovation, an advocacy group that works to build laws that support privacy, security, and STEM education. He also volunteers with the Geneva-based CyberPeace Institute as a Master CyberPeace Builder, providing free cybersecurity services to nongovernmental organizations (NGOs) that protect vulnerable communities around the world. Stephen can also be found volunteering with his son's Boy Scout troop, as well as camping and hiking with his wife and two children.

To contact USM Technology:
- E-mail: stephen.cracknell@usmtechnology.com
- Web: USMTechnology.com
- Phone: Dallas/Fort Worth: 214-390-9252; Greater Houston: 832-975-0035

CHAPTER 7

WHY CYBERCRIMINALS TARGET BUSINESSES LIKE YOURS

BY KONRAD MARTIN
Co-founder & CEO – Tech Advisors, Inc.

Small to medium-sized businesses (SMBs) face a lot of unique challenges with limited resources. Business owners need to constantly determine how to best use their resources to provide their products or services while meeting the legal, financial, and safety obligations placed on them. Modern businesses are now also faced with managing their use of networks and cybertools – in particular, the critical task of protecting the data stored and transmitted on those networks from cybercrime.

The problem is, SMBs tend to believe they are too small to be noticed by cybercriminals when, in fact, they are often the main targets. In 2020 alone, 48% of all successful cybercriminal hits were on SMBs of various sizes. Ironically, these businesses are often targeted because they believe they will not be attacked and therefore are not sufficiently protecting themselves or keeping up with IT security compliance. Additionally, SMBs are very often unaware of the types of threats that exist and how rapidly these threats change, much less what they should be doing to guard against the threats. Smart cybercriminals know that these businesses are often under-resourced, unaware, and unprotected, making them prime targets for an easy hit.

There are a lot of ways that SMBs can unknowingly leave themselves exposed to attacks. Here is a list of some of the most common security weaknesses:

1. **No written information security plan (WISP).** Much like HR documents that explain policies and procedures to prevent and respond to dangers such as an intruder or fire, this document sets out rules and regulations for employees to follow for IT security and how to prevent the breach of personally identifiable information (PII).

2. **Inadequate firewall protection.** Firewalls are a basic cybersecurity measure that most companies have in place; however, it takes a knowledgeable expert to determine if the firewalls are set up correctly and adequately. A poorly set-up firewall is a disaster waiting to happen.

3. **Allowing employees to search the web and visit unauthorized websites.** As we will discuss later, employees are often targeted by cybercriminals as a way to get into companies' databases. Allowing unauthorized web surfing creates a huge hole in security.

4. **Allowing employees to use unsecured personal devices (laptops, smartphones, tablets, desktops, etc.).** This is another good example of how a company may be creating a hole in its security. It is especially counterproductive if personal devices are being used in an attempt to cut business expenses. Any personal devices being used on the company's network need to be completely secured because any device is a potential door to the network itself. Businesses should think about implementing a bring your own device (BYOD) policy and limit the use of the company network to systems that have been approved by the IT team.

5. **Inadequate employee training**. Even though the people inside a company can be the biggest security liability, they are also one of the best assets for maintaining security within your organization. Thorough employee training equips each individual with the tools they need to stay suspicious and catch threats before those threats become breaches. Employee training comes in a stack of products, such as simulated phishing, short videos about security, and articles designed to show the employee how hacks happen and how best to avoid them.

6. **Inadequate monitoring and testing of employee training**. An important facet of employee training is regular monitoring and testing to ensure that the knowledge being given is also being understood, retained, and used. Regular testing, such as simulated phishing tests and penetration tests, can help show where education needs to be enhanced or where concepts need to be explained more thoroughly.

7. **Inadequate monitoring and testing of security measures**. Every single piece that makes up an entire security plan needs to be constantly monitored and regularly tested. When this is neglected, your organization can very quickly fall out of compliance and experience a breach.

8. **Using legacy software**. SMBs are more likely to use older versions of operating systems with the idea, "If it ain't broke, don't fix it." This is very dangerous. Software developers will abandon older operating systems, leaving them wide open to hacks. This means outdated software that is no longer supported can create gaping holes in security. It is important to keep all software updated to the most recent versions.

Many of the items on this list, if overlooked or mishandled, will not only leave your company open to attack but also push you out of compliance with security protocols and put you at risk for penalties and fees. HIPAA penalties alone can be $25,000 to $1.5 million per incident, in addition to incalculable damages to individuals whose PII may have been taken and used in the breach. Penalties due to the General Data Protection Regulation (GDPR) are 3% of your gross revenue or $25 million, whichever is higher. Obviously, these laws are written mainly as guardrails for big companies like Google. But the laws, and the penalties, do not change for smaller companies. Basic compliance is also a standard requirement for cyber liability insurance (CLI), which is absolutely essential. If basic compliance has not been maintained or cannot be proven, the insurance policy will likely deny coverage in the case of a loss, or you may not be issued a policy at all.

Also, notice that more than half of this list involves educating and training your personnel, from owners and management to entry-level employees. Bringing your employees together as a well-educated team that is equipped against attacks is the best way to prevent a dangerous breach. More about how to achieve this will be discussed later in this chapter.

Cybercrime changes constantly and rapidly, and it is often misunderstood by the very people it exploits. Many business owners do not realize that cybercriminals are highly intelligent and heavily resourced. Any tool that a business can access and use, such as a strong, high-quality firewall, is already owned by the criminals, and they already know a way around it. This is one of many reasons it is not enough to simply upgrade to more expensive tools and software. Effective security requires a holistic view of all potential entry points, not just quality equipment.

As mentioned above, one very large and overlooked entry point is knowledge of the employees themselves. Cybercriminals know that the easiest way into any organization, no matter how secure, is through its employees – human beings who can be tricked and manipulated. And since cybersecurity training for employees is often one of the weak points for SMBs, this is a popular path toward a breach. Criminals will often structure an attack around a single person inside the company, gathering information about that person to craft an approach that will work. Then, either the employee mistakenly hands over the information the thief wants, or the thief gains access to a device or network through which they can encrypt and copy data and hold that data ransom. Once this happens, acquiring the encryption key usually involves paying the criminals with a cybercurrency such as Bitcoin.

Criminals can take several approaches when manipulating people inside a company. One approach is to appear as a trustworthy source, and to do that, they need information on the person they are tricking. This is often easily gathered through employees' private social media accounts, particularly if security measures aren't adopted. There are 600,000 security hacks on Facebook every day. Most hacks, particularly in social media, are so common that they barely make the news. Each social media hack can hand a cybercriminal lots of information about that person and how to trick them into revealing usernames and passwords for the company network.

Another approach criminals take to exploit the people inside a company is to target certain businesses during their known busy seasons, when everyone's guard is down, and they're moving too quickly to double-check everything. This could be a CPA firm during tax season, retail giants during holidays, schools in August, and many other opportunities created by well-known seasonal patterns of business.

As a firm comprised of IT security consultants, Tech Advisors sees breaches performed through the manipulation of individuals on a constant basis. One client, a CFA named Tom, received an e-mail from one of his clients stating that he would be stopping by with a check to add to his personal portfolio. The e-mail was sent to the CFA's assistant, "Laurie," who responded that she was on vacation and unable to meet him at the office and asked if he could please fill out a wire transfer, which she attached. He agreed and sent the very large amount of money via the transfer

"Laurie" provided. Two weeks later, when the client saw that his portfolio still had not grown, he called Tom. Tom had no idea what his client was talking about – not only did the CFA company not allow the use of wire transfers with clients, but his assistant Laurie had never left town, and in fact, had not taken a vacation in over six months. By the time it was discovered that the real Laurie's Office 365 e-mail had been hacked, the client's money had been wired off to the hackers and was long gone.

It is important to note that the CFA's client had no reason to think Laurie's account had been hacked. However, this is a good example of why it is important to remain suspicious and double-check everything, particularly when dealing with proprietary information or large amounts of money. You should never transfer money or personal information without first calling the person requesting the information. Another lesson to be learned here is that it is not only software that thieves are trying to get past – it's people. That's why education is so critical. This situation also shows that there are many instances in which it is in the company's best interest to educate their clients thoroughly on the security policies in place for communicating and conducting transactions, so the client knows to be suspicious of anything that falls outside those policies.

Of course, SMBs have only so many resources. Because they are also the main target for cyberattacks, it can feel like a losing game to try to protect your business. It's hard to go to work every day, run your business and also have to worry about whether the software patches are current or the firewalls are adequate. The good news is that there is one real key to achieving and maintaining security: making sure your money is being spent in the right places, so the resources available to you are utilized to their utmost without breaking the bank. The security of your networks is not the place to cut corners, but it is still possible to spend efficiently.

In order to spend money on the right resources, it is essential to have the services of an expert third-party IT security consultant. This is also the most efficient way to achieve full compliance and maintain security monitoring. Security standards are being updated constantly as cybercriminal activity changes and adapts. A third-party consultant will take care of constantly monitoring the security guidelines that apply to your company for updates and changes, and then implementing those changes in your security, so you never fall out of compliance. This protects your company both from cyberattacks as well as penalties and fees.

These companies are also invested in continuing education for their employees as part of their business expenses, so they remain experts in their field. This means that contracting with a professional third-party organization not only costs less but also offers higher quality protection than an internal hire.

The serious reality of cybercrime is that it is not a matter of if a breach will happen to your business, but when. Even if your company is well within compliance with a great third-party contractor, breaches are still possible and can happen. The most important thing to remember is to focus on educating the people within your company and never resort to punishing or degrading employees who make mistakes. Everyone will make mistakes. Building up your team and creating strong loyalty is the best barrier to protect your business and all the information inside.

About Konrad

Konrad Martin is the CEO of Tech Advisors (https://tech-adv.com), a firm he founded in 2002 with his brother Kevin. Mr. Martin is a nationally recognized authority in the field of cybersecurity, and recently enjoyed a major role in the documentary, *Cyber Crime 2: The Dark Web Uncovered*. The film chronicles the growing plague of cybercrime, where billions of dollars are stolen or lost each year, destroying businesses and lives. Mr. Martin and nine other national cybersecurity experts were selected for the film, in which they explore the psychology and techniques of cybercrime and offer tips on how to avoid becoming a victim.

Under Mr. Martin's leadership, Tech Advisors has gained recognition as a leading technology solutions provider for small to mid-sized businesses. He has guided Tech Advisors onto the national stage through a variety of strategies: adding services, expanding beyond their original client base of CPAs into other industries, and offering cloud-based platform solutions for clients. His relationships with national cloud providers – including OS-33, Coaxis, and Microsoft Cloud Platform – enhance Tech Advisors' strong position in the marketplace. Tech Advisors was also selected as a "Fast Fifty" company by the *Boston Business Journal*, honored as one of the 50 fastest-growing private businesses in the Boston market.

Mr. Martin is the author of two books on cybersecurity. The first, *The IT Factor*, is a comprehensive guide for the small business owner who seeks to find a professional, competent IT provider. The second, *Hacked!*, offers strategies for staying one step ahead of cybercriminals. Additionally, Mr. Martin has authored articles on cybersecurity for a number of regional and national magazines. He has also been featured in *MSP Success Magazine*'s Spring 2021 Special Edition with his article, "The CPA Turned IT Consultant Every CPA Firm Wants To Know."

As a trusted advisor to the Massachusetts Society of CPAs, Konrad uses his publications and other platforms to educate audiences in the field of cybersecurity and the reality that cybercrime is a sophisticated and organized industry. He believes strongly that education and empathy are critical, and teams that are unified and knowledgeable are the best way to fight against the growing danger. A former CPA, he also wrote the WISP (written information security plan) for the Massachusetts Society of CPAs and its hundreds of members.

The Bangor, Maine, native enjoys an active "out of office" life as well. His non-IT hobbies include traveling, golfing, and athletic competitions. He is a nationally ranked swimmer, going back to his undergraduate days at the University of Maine. He likes hiking, triathlons, and a number of other challenging outdoor activities. As a family side note, his late father, J. Normand Martin, was an artist who designed the Paul Bunyan statue in Bangor; his artwork hangs in the State House in Augusta, Maine. Konrad Martin lives in Medway, Massachusetts, with his wife, Jeannie. They are parents to Rebecca, Adam, and Fritz.

For more information, contact Tech Advisors:
- E-mail: konradm@tech-adv.com
- Web: https://tech-adv.com/ or https://www.linkedin.com/company/tech-advisors-inc/
- Phone: 508-356-5565

CHAPTER 8

HOW TO PROTECT YOUR NETWORK IN A BYOD ENVIRONMENT

BY MICHAEL DUKE
Owner & Founder –
Just Smart Business Technologies, Inc.

Personal smartphones, tablets, and laptops have been regulars at workplaces for more than a decade. They have been tasked with being diverse in functionality – like the mullet of the device world. To keep that business up-front and secure and still allow the freedoms of the back-of-the-head party, companies started to establish bring-your-own-device (BYOD) policies. As the practice grew, it was necessary to formally set expectations for both the organization and the individual.[1]

DEVICE AT WORK VS. DEVICE FOR WORK

Whether your company allows personal devices to access the network or simply permits employees and guests to use them for Internet access and personal communications, you'll need to set up proper safety mechanisms. To secure the more limited *device at work* model, one approach is to segment the wireless network

---

1. Lyle Del Vecchio (2021, July 15), "What Is Bring Your Own Device (BYOD)?" *Planergy Blog: Business Strategy*, https://planergy.com/blog/what-is-byod/

and grant access only with a password. And for a more stringent level of safety, set minimum operating system and antivirus software requirements and consistently update them.

Device for work is the model in which employees use a personal device to conduct all their job duties. In terms of security considerations, they will need to access the corporate network to reach company applications, files, and e-mail, so segmentation will not suffice. It will be necessary to implement a more intensive safety plan.

PANDEMIC-INDUCED BYOD CULTURE

In 2020, when the Covid-19 pandemic accelerated work from home (WFH) culture, employees who didn't already have a remote set-up, needed computers, but just as demand skyrocketed, electronics manufacturing in China simultaneously halted or shut down completely. Companies and educational institutions rushed to purchase any available laptops and tablets, and quickly wiped-out inventory. In order for the workflow to continue, these organizations had no choice but to allow employees to use whatever personal devices they had at home.[2]

This meant that data was no longer protected behind commercial-grade firewalls. Instead, the corporate network was extended to the home, which typically has an insufficient level of security for business data needs. Most home routers have some type of firewall, but the processor speed only accommodates video streaming or gaming at best.[3]

Another concern was that companies had not prepared proper WFH policies or management tools. Employees did not know

---

2. Sarah Needleman & Aaron Tilley (2020, March 18), "Store Shelves Stripped Of Laptops As Coronavirus Increases Working From Home," *Wall Street Journal*, https://www.wsj.com/articles/store-shelves-stripped-of-laptops-as-coronavirus-increases-working-from-home-11584534112

3. Jason Perlow (2020, December 10), "Safer Networks At Home: Working Remotely In 2021," ZDNet, https://www.zdnet.com/article/safer-networks-at-home-working-remotely-in-2021/

what was expected of them, so they were more likely to make security-risky mistakes.

At this point, employers had two options. They could embrace BYOD and create policies and security measures to make it a safe practice. Or they could prohibit BYOD entirely and find a way to enforce the ban. Most had their hands tied, though, due to the computer shortage.

CREATING A BYOD POLICY

The increase in BYOD proliferation necessitated by the global health crisis makes it more crucial than ever for enterprise-level and small to medium-sized businesses (SMB) alike to know the potential risks and effective safety measures to mitigate them. When your organization adopts BYOD, you will need to create a policy to establish system maintenance measures and employee guidelines that reduce the chance of introducing unnecessary vulnerabilities into the company network and data while respecting the privacy of your team.

The first step in developing the BYOD policy is to reach out to your people. Survey employees to find out which personal devices they use, the applications they need to do their jobs and any accessibility assistance requirements. Ask for their perspectives on the advantages and disadvantages of using personal devices for work. Also, learn about their privacy concerns. Everyone will be affected by the rules and regulations, so it's important to gather and embrace input from all departments and seniority tiers to create an effective policy that represents the company as a whole.

While corporate management is essential to the planning process, if guidelines are blindly determined based solely on the company's high-level interests, they may be restrictive or fail to offer support for the technology employees use daily. This shortsighted approach inevitably damages morale and leads to a lack of employee participation, which wastes the resources invested in development.

BYOD POLICY CONTENTS

While policies may require additional provisions based on industry, any well-defined policy will include these essentials:

(a). Acceptable uses

Some of these items may seem like common sense but put them in writing anyway to protect the company from liability should an employee commit a violation.

- Permitted applications and assets
- Forbidden usage: e.g., devices may not be used while driving or operating any motorized vehicle, or in hazardous workspaces
- Conditions of applicable local, state, and federal laws and regulations

(b). Minimum device security requirements

In a survey conducted by Beyond Entity, shockingly, fewer than half the people who use only personal devices for work reported that their employer takes care of security measures.[4]

- Approved current operating systems (OS): e.g., Windows 10, Apple IOS not older than one version behind
- Antivirus software specifications
- Guidelines for strong passwords
- Two-factor authentication requirements
- Procedures for company installation of patches, updates, and other components, such as SSL certificates
- Mobile device security application requirements

---

4. Beyond Identity Blog (2021, May 28), "BYOD: Exploring The Evolution Of Work Device Practices In A New Remote-Forward Era" [Survey], https://www.beyondidentity.com/blog/byod-exploring-evolution-work-device-practices-survey

(c). Company rights

- Device alteration authority: e.g., remote wiping if lost or stolen
- Methods used to monitor and preserve communications conducted using the company networks

(d). Ownership of apps and data, defined

- Reimbursement policies: e.g., standard monthly fee, the cost of certain applications, or a portion of the monthly bill
- Departure expectations: e.g., will they be required to wipe their entire device or only the company data?

POLICY IMPLEMENTATION

Once your organization has created your BYOD policy, you need provisions to hold employees accountable. Without known disciplinary action for failing to abide, your policy has no clout. Describe in detail how you will measure and enforce the rules.

IT MANAGEMENT RESPONSIBILITIES

Locking down security while ensuring user privacy is a balancing act that your IT team or managed services provider (MSP) must face. Fortunately, mobile device management (MDM) systems can help. And while they previously accommodated only enterprise-level organizations, these tools are now available for organizations with 100 or fewer users.

What can MDM systems do for you? They can support containerization, secure corporate e-mail and documents, and enforce corporate policies. If a portion of a device is essentially segregated into its own protected area, you can assign a separate set of policies that differ from those that apply to the rest of the applications and content on the device.

When a user is logged in to the containerized area, they use a separate password and cannot access personal apps and other features outside the container. This practice limits corporate liability without impacting personal use. The downside is it does not protect employees' personal data on devices that are lost, so they must be wiped. However, the erasure can easily be mitigated with proper personal backups.

Containerization is one way to prevent employees from feeling like company restrictions infringe on their personal freedoms. The separate areas allow them to safely download applications on their own device and other behaviors not permitted on the business side.

The IT team or MSP should also deliver updates over-the-air (OTA), aka wirelessly. To ensure that personal devices are kept up-to-date and compliant with company protocols, automate updates OTA. This applies to VPN and WiFi profiles, credentials, and apps needed to access work such as e-mail programs, contacts, and calendars.[5]

IT will also need to encrypt sensitive data both at rest and in transit to ensure that the content is protected even if a device is stolen, or the data is intercepted over an unsecured network. They may take advantage of built-in device and operating system controls to manage the safety of installed apps. Apple IOS devices can be configured in such a way that denies access to the app store, and for Android devices, Android Enterprise is available to manage the Google Play portal so it contains only approved apps.

Make sure you are able to keep track of which devices are connected to your network. Set up applications that detect a new phone, laptop, et al. so you can automatically apply management tools that protect the system. If you are unable to institute the necessary protocols, you may have to resort to blocking the account altogether.[5]

5. IBM Security (2020, July) "10 Rules for BYOD IBM Corporation," https://www.ibm.com/downloads/cas/YK52D6GD

Always be considerate of your users. Take time and convenience into account when devising your device enrollment plan. Offer ways to self-enroll, which streamlines the process and does not detract from the IT team's workload. Consider using Google Android Enterprise zero-touch enrollment and the Apple Device Enrollment Program (DEP) for automation. Also, set up systems that allow users to reset a password, find a device, or wipe it without help-desk assistance.[5]

Encourage employees to monitor data usage and use WiFi when possible to keep costs down. Consider instituting a policy to minimize data overages.[5]

HOW DO YOU KNOW IF BYOD IS RIGHT FOR YOUR ORGANIZATION?

Allowing personal devices to be used to conduct work or even simply to access the Internet at the workplace provides myriad benefits for the company and employees. However, implementing a BYOD program is tricky. And the challenges can multiply in a multi-platform environment.

When contemplating instituting a BYOD policy, identify and assess potential privacy and security risks such as personal identifiable information (PII) like name, address, or social security number. It's also important to examine costs in terms of both the human and financial resources needed to implement, monitor, and update all aspects of the program.

Analyze which combinations of technological and policy solutions are best for your company. The complexity of a BYOD program lies in the integration of both personal and enterprise applications and data within a single device.

You may find, as Beyond Identity did when surveying more than 1,000 employees, that those using only a personal device for work "were actually the most likely to rate their productivity as 'excellent.'" This argument was supported by benefits such as streamlined work and personal activities, with everything they need "being in one place." Also, they were able to avoid learning curves when asked to switch to a device chosen by the employer.[4]

If you do choose to put a BYOD program in place, implement it on a case-by-case basis for particular user groups, like the IT, HR, or sales department. Test it out to demonstrate that it safely, securely, and responsibly addresses each team's needs.

BYOD security requires a multifaceted approach that protects against cyber-attackers while minimizing intrusions on employees' privacy and personal use. If BYOD is done right and you effectively mitigate security risks, your organization can reap its rewards. Follow a responsible BYOD plan and enjoy lower hardware and software costs, and a team that experiences greater work-life balance, productivity and, as a result, satisfaction. On the plus side, companies benefit from reduced hardware and software costs, while employees benefit from increased productivity. It can be a win-win for both sides.

Sources
1. Lyle Del Vecchio (2021, July 15), "What Is Bring Your Own Device (BYOD)?" *Planergy Blog: Business Strategy*, https://planergy.com/blog/what-is-byod/
2. Sarah Needleman & Aaron Tilley (2020, March 18), "Store Shelves Stripped Of Laptops As Coronavirus Increases Working From Home," *Wall Street Journal*, https://www.wsj.com/articles/store-shelves-stripped-of-laptops-as-coronavirus-increases-working-from-home-11584534112
3. Jason Perlow (2020, December 10), "Safer Networks At Home: Working Remotely In 2021," *ZDNet*, https://www.zdnet.com/article/safer-networks-at-home-working-remotely-in-2021/
4. Beyond Identity Blog (2021, May 28), "BYOD: Exploring The Evolution Of Work Device Practices In A New Remote-Forward Era" [Survey], https://www.beyondidentity.com/blog/byod-exploring-evolution-work-device-practices-survey
5. IBM Security (2020, July) "10 Rules for BYOD IBM Corporation," https://www.ibm.com/downloads/cas/YK52D6GD

About Michael

Michael Duke has demonstrated a lifelong love for being on the move, so it is no surprise that he is interested in mobile technology. As a kid, he biked through the neighborhood, tossing newspapers onto driveways, and in high school, he picked up pizzas and drove them to the homes of hungry folks. He once worked as a city bus driver and was so good at his job that he won first place at the International Bus Roadeo in North America, a contest that proves one's prowess behind the wheel.

He later became an owner-operator long-haul trucker and says that on the road he had time to think about his fascination with the power of math and computations. He took his affinity for reading manuals to the classroom, where he studied information technology. A professor commended his knowledge and connected him with a program at UCLA to earn a community-college-level teaching credential. He then had the opportunity to apply both his computer science and transportation industry knowledge when he was hired as the IT director for a trucking company.

Michael enjoys continuing with his education and has earned professional development credentials. He is a Microsoft Certified Systems Engineer (MCSE) and holds a Cisco Express Foundation Field Specialist Certification.

Back in 1988, Michael started Just Smart Business Technologies (JSBT) to serve small to mid-sized businesses in the region of Southern California known as the Inland Empire. JSBT provides fully managed IT services that solve business problems, with an emphasis on cyber security. The company is founded on a belief in integrity, honesty, respect, and the importance of fostering joy for the work and people they serve. He and his team also cultivate an environment that encourages creative thinking. It is important to the company that their technicians avoid "geek-speak" when talking with clients and, instead, choose relatable language.

Always in motion, Michael and his wife often travel across the US via motorhome and train. They especially love trips that include their three daughters, six grandchildren, and four great-grandchildren.

Michael has never flown an airplane but hopes to see the country from the pilot's seat one day. (We can't confirm or deny that his beagle Marley and best friend Cleo the ragdoll cat may have planted this idea while watching Snoopy pretend to be the World War 1 Flying Ace.)

Michael's hero is Black NASA scientist Katherine Johnson, who calculated the trajectory for *Apollo 11* to reach the moon and safely return to earth. Her job title was "computer" back before we had machines to assist with mathematics. He says, "It's incredible to think of the capability of the human mind. Sure, computers today need to be programmed by humans, but for a person to do the math by hand and get a rocket to launch and land at a specific destination is astounding."

Contact Michael:
Just Smart Business Technologies, Inc.
Murrieta, CA
- E-mail: mduke@justsb.com
- Web: https://www.justsb.com
- Phone: 951-968-7066

CHAPTER 9

CRITICAL STEPS TO TAKE IF YOU'VE BEEN HACKED

BY MICHAEL D. MOORE
Founder & CEO – M3 Networks

Cybersecurity breaches are in the headlines constantly. They have become so common, most of them don't even make it to the news. The potential of a business experiencing a breach has evolved from a question of "if" to a question of "when." And when that "when" comes, there are some critical steps that absolutely cannot be overlooked.

To start, *how* we think of breaches is very important. Often, people overuse the words "data" and "network" when they should really be thinking in terms of "business," "family," and "money." This is really important. People so often think: "My data has been affected." No – your *money* has been affected. When you start thinking of it in terms of: "My family's personal information has been leaked, and they are targeting my life," that's very different than, "Our company policy got leaked on the dark web." The word "data" is vague and abstract. It's important to think of these things in concrete terms of impact.

I once had a guy in a webinar ask me: "My company is quite small.

Can't I just shut down my company if something happens?" I replied, "I think that's a question for your wife. Is she going to be super happy that you gave up your entire income just because you had a network breach, and you were unprepared?" This man's question showed that he wasn't thinking of the real impact of his decision to remain unprotected. A breach is an impactful event, and it's important to think of it in terms that reflect that.

IT security professionals can help answer questions about your security, but we can't provide the motivation to actually take the right steps. That's like asking a personal trainer to convince you to get in shape. It's not their job to make you want to train—it's their job to train you if *you* want to.

So, what should you do when this happens to you? Here is a list of critical steps to take:

1. *Involve the experts.* A lot of times, when people are sick, they go on WebMD. Don't do that—call the doctor. Like your physical health, your business' health needs to be handled in the same way: professionally. And there's more than one professional that needs to be included. If you're going to win a football game, you need all the players: a running back, a quarterback, an offensive line, etc., and each of them is pretty useless without the others. The foundational players you'll need on your cybersecurity team are:

   • A specialized cyber-attorney on retainer. The attorney functions similarly to a weatherman – they keep track of what is coming before it comes. They are negotiating for you constantly. This cannot be a general attorney; it must be someone who specializes in cybercrime.
   • An IT firm that has specific cybersecurity expertise. They will be your first responders and the remediation crew after a breach. They will also be the ones to help you set up preventative measures to mitigate your company's risk, as well as a thorough protocol to follow in every possible situation.

A while back, we had a prospective client who received our proposal for cybersecurity services and IT support and replied, "It's too expensive." We actually hear this a lot. So, I told this client the same thing I have told others: "The pain you'll feel for not making a good decision now will be much greater than any possible regret for investing in good protection." About a year later, almost to the day, this company was being promoted on a national talk show. It was the worst time in the world for them to have a security issue – they were selling products like crazy from the promotions, and they were refreshing their inventory as fast as they could. Sure enough, they got hacked, and the company accounts were drained. All the money was gone. They were calling us in a panic, asking what they should do. We worked with the company, we worked with the FBI, and we got all their money back.

We've seen this same story played out a million times in a million different ways. A client doesn't want to move forward with preventative protections, usually because they think it's too expensive. But then they have a breach, and they learn that what they *really* can't afford is a devastating loss to their business.

2. *Remain calm.* Imagine you are the leader of your company, and your area had a tornado coming. If you start screaming, "We're all going to die!" you won't be helping anything. One of the most important things for executives and leaders of companies to learn is to treat their employees kindly, especially during a breach. Be more kind and calm than you've ever been. As the leader of a company, it is time to have the calm 'game face.' Nobody gets to own the big chair and then complain that they have to lead people.

Believe it or not, this actually comes into play long before a breach even occurs. Imagine if you were in a family dynamic, and you told everyone to leave you alone and never tell you about their problems. Then imagine they had a huge problem that was going to evaporate all of your finances. They wouldn't feel they could come to you for help because you told them not to, and now they're afraid of you. You need to keep that open line of communication. Because one day, someone is going to get a phishing email, and they're not going to want to bother you to ask about it, so they're going to click through it and enter all the credentials just in case it's genuine. Then all the money is gone, and you're left with a mess.

3. *Follow* <u>exactly</u> *what your experts tell you to do.* Your IT cybersecurity team will have helped you put together a plan to follow in case anything happens. Pull out this plan and follow it exactly. After notifying the correct authorities, your IT security team should be your first call – do not touch anything until they tell you. They will tell you whether you need to: 1) start mitigating, 2) restore from backups, or 3) do nothing because your forensic experts may need that data. *Do not delete the evidence.* They will likely have you call your legal team to advise whether to call local authorities or the FBI (most often, it's the FBI).

It is crucial to trust your IT company with the administrator/ elevated credentials and never give them to the company executives. Typically, executives want these credentials because they want to be able to fire others without concern for the access. However, the truth is that executives are typically the worst at managing their credentials.

A few years ago, a client called to let us know that they had hired an in-house IT director. He was an employee who was originally in another position and was terrible at it, so they gave him the position of IT director. He was just supposed to manage the company's relationship with us and nothing else. They called and asked us to give him the administrative credentials. Three days later, they called again to say that their entire network was completely encrypted. It didn't take much detective work to figure out how it happened – the new employee-turned-IT-director called immediately after. He explained that there was a weird file on the network that had been on his thumb drive titled "porn.exe" and that he kept clicking it, and each time, different colors and files flashed up on the screen. He wanted to know what he should do. This new director was the attack vector destroying all of the network data. My team worked for about three days straight, night and day, cleaning up all of the damage. The administrative credentials should never be in the hands of anyone outside of your IT team – everyone else is a liability.

4. *Always assume that the criminal is a well-organized machine that aims to do you more damage.* Don't just relax after the damage has been cleaned up. Always assume that the criminal who has done damage to your company has targeted you specifically and will do further damage to you. Eighty-five percent of companies that sustain a breach will get hacked again – not always by the same people.

I've been an avid, terrible fisherman since I was about five years old. You could take me fishing, and we could sit by the dock for five hours, but I won't catch anything. However, I recently went on a guided fishing tour on a lake, and I learned one key thing: with a guide, I can catch a lot of fish because they take you out to the right spots. I caught about 20 fish. I learned that all of the guides speak over radio and tell each other where to go, and all the guides' boats end up in exactly the same place. That's what the hackers do when they find out you've been breached: they all call each other, just like those fishing guides do, and say, "This is where the fish are, come get it." Just like that, you've just become their honeypot. It's similar to a teenager finding out where the party is: they tell everyone. They spread the word about which company was hit, exactly where (or who) the vulnerability is, how to get in, etc. The second breach may not be the same people, but it will happen because of that initial breach.

It is also important to note that the average cyber-attack event happens 9 to 18 months after some sort of compromise has occurred. That means that the criminals are lurking that whole time on your network, building a case for themselves on how much damage they can do, where they hit, and how. The big thing they will learn is how much your cyber liability insurance policy deductible is. They will pick a monetary amount slightly lower than that, then attack with ransomware. For instance, say your deductible is $20,000. They will attack with ransomware and demand $15,000. They know you won't put in a claim and pay the deductible of $20,000 when you could pay them $15,000.

A while back, we performed an audit for a prospective customer, and in our report, we suggested that they enable two-factor authentication on their email. They were afraid it would be expensive and said they didn't want to "invest" in that. Not long after, an employee went to the CFO on a Friday because he did not receive his direct deposit. The CFO showed him the pay stub proving that the deposit had gone through and then mentioned casually that he was surprised the employee had emailed last week with new checking and routing numbers, but he made sure they were updated for his paycheck. The employee replied that he never sent new checking and routing numbers. The employee's email had been hacked, and his paycheck was long gone. The hacker had been lurking around to figure out who had a bigger paycheck, who was more gullible, and who the CFO would trust.

Because repeat attacks are so common, after any breach, it is critical to behave as if you have an incredibly infectious disease. People often make the misstep of thinking that everything will be fine, and that they'll just pay their cyber liability deductible and move on with their lives. But until the root cause of the problem is resolved and every test is clear, you must act as if you are still infected and stay hypervigilant in the future.

All the steps above are crucial to take after sustaining any type of breach or hack. However, after the mess has been cleaned up and the dust settles, the most important step to take moving forward is to stay suspicious. Double-check everything. Educate your team, stay kind and compassionate with them, and ensure that they feel comfortable having open discussions with you about their work problems. Never take a shortcut – if a login or password is convenient for you, it's convenient for a hacker. Involve *all* the experts. Cybersecurity is not just about computers – it's about keeping people and their livelihoods safe.

About Michael

Michael D. Moore is the founder and CEO of M3 Networks, based in Fort Worth, Texas. Michael first became interested in IT at the age of 12 when his paternal grandfather took him to Infomart, the world's first and only information processing marketing center, in Dallas, Texas. Michael continued to dabble with building computers and teaching himself how to code while working various jobs through college. In 2001, at the time of the terrorist attacks, Michael was working at American Airlines. In the aftermath of 9/11, Michael was laid off. He was hired by his first technology company later that year and began learning everything he could. He mentored under an Army Ranger who trained him in CISCO and Microsoft, trading tech lessons for joint workout sessions.

He later moved on to work at a managed service provider and later served as an in-house IT director for a large oil and gas firm. Over the years, he found that there was a need for a higher level of customer service in the IT sphere and that he had a heart for delivering a passionate level of empathy to the customer base. He enjoyed the work he was doing, but he knew he needed to find a way to impact more businesses and teach others along the way.

In 2008, M3 Networks was born from those passions. Over the years, his company has expanded from basic help desk support to offering a full range of managed IT and cybersecurity services. In 2019, M3 Networks appeared on CRN Network's "2019 Managed Service Provider 500," an annual list that compiles the United States' most innovative solution providers.

Today, M3 Networks still functions with the power of Michael's passion for empathetic and excellent customer service, evidenced by a nearly perfect customer satisfaction rate. Their satisfied clients range across the US. His team remains on the cutting edge of their field, and they strive to share their knowledge with their clients and the community. Michael and his team partner regularly with charity efforts in their local community, continually finding new ways to focus on helping people. M3 Networks continues to grow as a "service first" company that does justice to the heart of the owner.

You can reach Michael at:
- E-mail: mmoore@m3networks.com
- LinkedIn: https://www.linkedin.com/in/themikedmoore
- Web: https://www.m3networks.com
- Office Phone: 817-500-5945
- Text: 817-968-7063

CHAPTER 10

WHY IS HIPAA COMPLIANCE IMPORTANT?

BY PAUL TRACEY
Founder, Owner, and CEO – Innovative Technologies

The Health Insurance Portability and Accountability Act of 1996 (HIPAA), which was designed to protect the privacy of patient records, is actually an excellent framework for any organization's security plan. It not only addresses technical measures needed to control the physical environment but also emphasizes the administrative processes necessary to secure data.

And the HIPAA Security Rule, first enforced in 2005, is truly the gold standard for security and should be applied across all industries. The Centers for Disease Control and Prevention (CDC) issued it to provide the following guidelines for electronically protected health information (e-PHI):

- Ensure the confidentiality, integrity, and availability of all e-PHI.
- Detect and safeguard against anticipated threats to the security of information.
- Protect against anticipated, impermissible uses or disclosures.
- Certify compliance by the workforce.

Back in 2003, HIPAA was enforced only in the medical field, but financial industries were also held to HIPAA regulations due to their access to protected health information during the accounting processes. In fact, all business associates of a HIPAA-covered entity are subject to compliance. This includes vendors such as a cleaning service that works in facilities where records are stored.[1]

It is refreshing that both California and New York have passed laws for all businesses that mirror many of the core principles in HIPAA. And more states and industries are certain to follow this trend. However, it is crucial for your organization to implement tight safety protocols long before you are legally required to do so. You can't afford to wait the three to five years it takes from proposal to enforcement. Always follow stricter safety policies than the law dictates.[2,3]

Remember, vehicles in the United States weren't even required to include seat belts until 1968. And it took more than 15 years for New York to lead the path and pass the first usage mandate, which applied only to front-seat riders. Consider how many lives were lost while legislators were kicking around the concept of mandating seat belts.[4]

CONSEQUENCES OF NONCOMPLIANCE

Providers held to HIPAA regulations often don't realize that the fines for violations may be less severe if they have taken proper measures to comply, so it pays to make the effort. If a provider has properly trained an employee and received the policy attestation

1. Centers for Disease Control and Prevention (2005), Health Insurance Portability and Accountability Act of 1996 (HIPAA), https://www.cdc.gov/phlp/publications/topic/hipaa.html
2. State of California Department of Justice (2018), California Consumer Privacy Act (CCPA), https://www.oag.ca.gov/privacy/ccpa
3. New York State Senate (2019, May 7), Senate Bill S5575B, https://www.nysenate.gov/legislation/bills/2019/s5575
4. D. Sheldon (2021, June 9), "A Seat Belt History Timeline," *Your AAA*, https://magazine.northeast.aaa.com/daily/life/cars-trucks/a-seat-belt-history-timeline/

for the issue in question, the fine and/or associated legal actions can be greatly mitigated. However, if the violation is deemed negligent because training and policy were not in place, the fines can be ten times higher.

Each HIPAA violation can cost from $100 to $50,000, with maximum annual penalties of $1.5 million. The Department of Health and Human Services' Office for Civil Rights (OCR) has created a four-tier structure to determine liability, with level four being the most severe. Factors considered when assigning a tier also include an organization's willingness to cooperate to improve security, the number of people affected, types of data that were breached, and compliance history.[5]

Here are two examples of health care providers that were seriously burned by violations:

In 2019, Touchstone Medical Imaging paid a $3 million fine after OCR and the Federal Bureau of Investigations (FBI) discovered that 300,000 patients' e-PHI was visible online as search engines were able to index the data. The breach could have been prevented if the company put tighter security in place to protect just one server.[6]

In 2021, Excellus Health Plan settled at $5.1 million after hackers successfully used malware to expose e-PHI of 9.3 million people in Upstate New York. It stings a bit to know they are in our region, and we could have helped to prevent this – and for a lot less money![7]

In addition to the expense, noncompliance hurts your reputation.

5. Steve Alder (2021, January 15), "What Are The Penalties For HIPAA Violations?"- *HIPAA Journal*, https://www.hipaajournal.com/what-are-the-penalties-for-hipaa-violations-7096/
6. Jessica Kim Cohen (2019, May 6), "Medical Imaging Company To Pay $3 Million HIPAA Fine," *Modern Healthcare*, https://www.modernhealthcare.com/technology/medical-imaging-company-pay-3-million-hipaa-fine
7. US Department of Health & Human Services (2021, January 5), "Health Insurer Pays $5.1 Million To Settle Data Breach Affecting Over 9.3 Million People," press release, https://www.hhs.gov/about/news/2021/01/15/health-insurer-pays-5-1-million-settle-data-breach.html

Details of all violations permanently appear on the publicly available Wall of Shame. And a breach doesn't have to qualify as a HIPAA violation to be catastrophic. It may still result in data loss, costly downtime, and a ransom to pay.[8]

REASONS MANY COMPANIES DO NOT HAVE ADEQUATE CYBERSECURITY IN PLACE

Most companies that we initially speak to don't know what data they hold or where it's located in their systems. You can't possibly secure assets if you don't know your inventory and where it's stored.

Let's say someone bursts into a warehouse and steals $100K in motorcycle parts. The thief gets away with it because the boxes weren't properly labeled and never got logged into the system. Since the company didn't keep track of the merchandise, they never installed high-security locks and cameras to protect it.

Companies have misconceptions about which data is being protected. A client may tell us they store all their medical data in an electronic health records (EHR) program, then invite us to perform an audit. We scan their systems and assign a dollar value to the type and scope of e-PHI, then calculate a total liability. We find $2 million worth of medical information saved in downloads folders and other unencrypted locations – all outside the EHR.

And few companies have the time to conduct proper HIPAA assessments. Consider the small medical practices without any IT staff at all and only one office manager. The only HIPAA compliance this person has the bandwidth to do is to fill out the annual questionnaire.

Even in organizations large enough to have an internal IT department, employees are overwhelmed. In addition to their

---

8. Marlene M. Maheu (2021, Jun 10), "HIPAA Wall Of Shame: See Who Has Violated HIPAA," Telehealth.org, https://telehealth.org/hipaa-wall-of-shame/

regular responsibilities, they have to install patches to fix previously identified security holes. And they face the looming possibility of a new "Zero Day" attack, which can tie up the entire department for days or weeks.

There's also a lack of interest. Let's face it – the HIPAA packet is not making any summer beach read list. At 80 pages, how many employees take the time to review it, ask questions and ensure comprehension before signing their name to attest they've done those things? The executive director, legal staff, and a few board members might read the document, but do they ensure that everyone in the company knows their role in compliance? Not likely.

Cybersecurity inequity is highly problematic. Sadly, some organizations cannot afford essential IT services. On average, medical institutions allocate 7% to 10% of revenue to their tech budget. However, most educational institutions only spend 1% to 3% of revenue on technology resources. School budgets simply lack the funding to properly secure their networks. In 2020, grants were available for hardware expenses related to working and teaching from home, but the scope was limited and did not provide much relief. Compare this to the average 'tech spending' across all industries, which is 5%.

THE GREAT TECH CRUNCH OF 2020

If security measures were loosely followed before the pandemic, consider the disaster that began in March of 2020. When states, counties, cities – and even entire countries – issued stay-at-home orders to prevent the spread of Covid-19, we had insufficient time to prepare. The majority of workers with jobs that could be done remotely only had in-office setups, so there was a mad rush to get computers home and deployed. At first, due to high demand, it was difficult to even procure the equipment. There weren't enough chips, and PCs were on backorder. Supply chains could not keep up.

When chips were available, many of the urgently deployed work-from-home (WFH) computers were not set up with proper security, firewalls, or other protocols. And as often happens when pressed for time, many people skipped steps and made mistakes. No one expected perfection, though, because we had life and death on our minds. This is understandable, but as time goes on, the consequences will be catastrophic. Many companies are about to suffer big-time as a result of being in a rush to get s--t done. Sadly, the IT world's neglect is leading to its own self-inflicted global crisis.

No one was prepared for WFH en masse. As an increasing number of companies catch up with audits, we will inevitably learn that a ton of organizations did not give their employees secure home setups. I predict a giant spike in the number of dark web credentials that will be found over the next year. Note that there's a delay in the underworld too, so don't think you're in the clear just yet. If they got you in 2020, credentials such as usernames and passwords will eventually show up for sale.

Another problem with the instant shift away from the office environment was that companies didn't have WFH policies in place. Employees didn't know expectations for online behavior at the home office. They likely reverted to the relaxed mentality usually reserved for time away from work.

Many people tend to take only casual precautions while in their own space – even when using a work computer or connecting to a virtual machine via a personal device. Seemingly harmless actions may include quickly checking Amazon for the price of hiking shoes or hopping onto Facebook to send a birthday message. If non-work-related websites are not restricted, users could be vulnerable and end up visiting malicious sites.

Since a home network is not likely set up with corporate-level security, we are unable to detect or remediate threats that occur outside the office. Home Internet connections and public hotspots are typically unencrypted. They are also malicious, making everything you do visible to any hacker.

And cybercriminals loved the widespread surge in video conferencing and saw Zoom and Microsoft Teams with dollar signs in their eyes. They knew the hurriedly installed software was likely not secure. And while Zoom has since locked down security with serious upgrades, they were not ready for the staggering scale of usage. At first, it was riddled with porn pop-ups. (Try to explain that to a third-grader logged into a math lesson.)[9]

IMPLEMENT RULES AND TRAINING AND YOU WILL TRANSFORM THE COMPANY

It's amazing to watch a company's transformation after they adopt a new mindset. For one, the culture can be unrecognizable when you see shifts in employee computer behaviors.

Here's one example of a cultural problem I frequently observe. When I visit a prospect for an intro meeting, I like to chat with people at the company. I note how they refer to the computer they use. If they call it "my computer," this indicates a lack of understanding. It's not *your* computer. It's the agency's computer. It's not *your* data. It's the agency's data. Subconsciously – if you use a possessive regarding a piece of technology, what does your behavior look like?

If you borrow a friend's car, do you drive it with the same care as yours? No, you do not. I guarantee you are more careful. This is because someone else will scrutinize the vehicle to ensure you brought it back in the same condition. If you scratch your own bumper in the parking lot, the beef stays between you and the shopping cart.

---

9. Kari Paul (2021, April 20), "Zoom Releases Security Updates In Response To 'Zoom-Bombings,'" *The Guardian*, https://www.theguardian.com/technology/2020/apr/23/zoom-update-security-encryption-bombing

OUTSOURCE AN IT FIRM

Organizations simply do not have the hundreds of hours per year required to do HIPAA training and implementation correctly. We recognized this and realized we could provide a solution – a package that freed up clients' time. It allows the company to only allocate 15 to 20 hours per year to HIPAA compliance. We do the rest.

We run scans, install security mechanisms such as firewalls and antivirus software, create policy attestations and file reports. We hold training sessions. We even partner with a compliance group that offers audit response should they need it.

We also gamify our security practice. We send employees a three- to five-minute video with a cybersecurity TipTech and run analytics to find out how many people watched it. And we use a tool that simulates phishing attacks to catch dangerous employee behavior. If they click the link or download the file, they get locked out of their e-mail and are instantly enrolled in training. We let internal management know which employees are following safety protocol and putting in the time to learn from the videos, and ask them to recognize those people in front of others.

CONCLUSION

In general, the workforce is significantly undereducated about technology. More training is essential to prevent cybersecurity breaches. Most people do not realize how much time it takes to make sure a company is safe or that most internal IT departments are too busy to do the compliance work right.

Bottom line, you have to hire someone. I'm not here to do a sales pitch, but I'm here to let you know that you could lose everything if you blow off precautionary measures. You absolutely need to keep your data locked down. And there's no time to drag your feet. Please take cybersecurity seriously. And find at least one geek who is willing to read that 'damn' 80-page book and tell you all you need to know.

Sources

1. Centers for Disease Control and Prevention (2005), Health Insurance Portability and Accountability Act of 1996 (HIPAA), https://www.cdc.gov/phlp/publications/topic/hipaa.html
2. State of California Department of Justice (2018), California Consumer Privacy Act (CCPA), https://www.oag.ca.gov/privacy/ccpa
3. New York State Senate (2019, May 7), Senate Bill S5575B, https://www.nysenate.gov/legislation/bills/2019/s5575
4. D. Sheldon (2021, June 9), "A Seat Belt History Timeline," Your AAA, https://magazine.northeast.aaa.com/daily/life/cars-trucks/a-seat-belt-history-timeline/
5. Steve Alder (2021, January 15), "What Are The Penalties For HIPAA Violations?"- HIPAA Journal, https://www.hipaajournal.com/what-are-the-penalties-for-hipaa-violations-7096/
6. Jessica Kim Cohen (2019, May 6), "Medical Imaging Company To Pay $3 Million HIPAA Fine," Modern Healthcare, https://www.modernhealthcare.com/technology/medical-imaging-company-pay-3-million-hipaa-fine
7. US Department of Health & Human Services (2021, January 5), "Health Insurer Pays $5.1 Million To Settle Data Breach Affecting Over 9.3 Million People," press release, https://www.hhs.gov/about/news/2021/01/15/health-insurer-pays-5-1-million-settle-data-breach.html
8. Marlene M. Maheu (2021, Jun 10), "HIPAA Wall Of Shame: See Who Has Violated HIPAA," Telehealth.org, https://telehealth.org/hipaa-wall-of-shame/
9. Kari Paul (2021, April 20), "Zoom Releases Security Updates In Response To 'Zoom-Bombings,'" *The Guardian*, https://www.theguardian.com/technology/2020/apr/23/zoom-update-security-encryption-bombing

About Paul

Paul Tracey is the founder, owner, and CEO of Innovative Technologies. He has seen cybersecurity disasters he wishes he could 'unsee.' While at a large healthcare institution, he discovered the department head infected the whole place with malware via his personal laptop. One person made a single mistake, and it cost half a million dollars. Through this experience, he began to notice that while most companies may have some type of security protocol, when compliance interrupts expedience or convenience, managers circumvent the rules. If the organization is wealthy enough, in the event of a breach, they pay the fines, make minimal changes, and carry on.

Not all businesses, though, have the means to survive an attack financially. And the data loss alone is enough to sink them. They are more likely to end up like an engineer he met recently when buying his used office furniture. He was selling it all because he had to shut down his firm. He said, "Man, I wish I'd met you six months ago. We got hacked, and I had to close my business." The man had lost everything. Every day, sitting in a chair and at a desk, the man and his dismantled team no longer need the visceral and unsettling reminder of the cautionary tale that informs the reason Paul does this work.

You may wonder, how does a company go from thriving to bankrupt in a matter of months? Simply put, most organizations do not make time for security.

The fact that sizable organizations do not take cybersecurity seriously didn't sit well with Paul. And the imbalance that made it difficult for small to mid-sized entities to thrive was infuriating. He couldn't bear to stand by and watch them suffer. In turn, building on IT industry experience, studies in information technologies and business at SUNY Adirondack, he founded Innovative Technologies. His company provides technology solutions that minimize security risks for smaller health care providers and other SMBs in Greater Albany, New York.

Nearly a decade later, Innovative Technologies continues to help clients ensure they have security and compliance procedures in place and a well-trained staff. They have earned the reputation as a leading managed security services provider (MSSP) in Upstate New York.

Paul renews his HIPAA Seal of Compliance Verification annually and offers his knowledge as part of the company's compliance program. He is the author of *Delete The Hackers Playbook*, written to educate the public about ransomware, based on his success in protecting clients from falling victim to paying for data restoration. (https://www.upstatetechsupport.com/cybersecuritybook/)

In his community, Paul served the Glens Falls Greenjackets Semi-pro football team as chief technology officer and board member. Innovative Technologies sponsors the team and also donates annually to St. Jude's and several local nonprofits.

Profound honesty, transparency, and humility are values that permeate Paul's work. And the sign on his office wall, "Never Stop Auditing," applies beyond the literal to his practice of perpetually seeking solutions.

Contact:
Innovative Technologies
Malta, New York (Saratoga County)

- E-mail: info@upstatetechsupport.com
- Web: https://www.upstatetechsupport.com
- Phone: 518-900-7004

CHAPTER 11

INSURE YOUR COMPANY'S SAFETY AND WELL-BEING

BY SCOTT KREISBERG
Founder and Owner – One Step Secure IT Services

In the past couple of years, the number and frequency of cyber-attacks have skyrocketed. It is now no longer a question of whether your company will suffer an attack but rather when it will happen. Just as we protect our homes and health with insurance for when an issue will arise, it is essential to protect the security of our businesses. The time has passed that cyber liability insurance (CLI) is an extra bit of coverage to have, just in case. It has become an essential part of a functional business, and very often is the only thing that stands in the way of a breach decimating a business.

Without CLI, business owners are fully responsible for the entirety of a security event, as well as any consequences that follow. These consequences could include fines and penalties, forensic audits, public relations consultations, data restoration, reputation and client trust loss, lawsuits, and credit monitoring services for anyone whose information the breach compromised – all of this in addition to the company's own downtime and loss of income. In total, the cost of a data breach for a small business can easily shoot past several hundred thousand dollars. The deeper damage is almost incalculable, as successful cyber-attacks demolish your business's reputation and client trust, which inevitably results in additional business loss. In fact, 60% of small businesses close up shop within six months of a breach.

This is a universal danger that does not discriminate – but it does hunt for prey strategically. Although every business needs cyber liability insurance, criminals target small businesses more often simply because they tend to be easier hits. The year 2020 alone saw a 400% increase in cybercrime, with 43% of all cyber-attacks targeting small businesses and almost a third (28%) of data breaches involving small businesses. Cybercriminals know that small businesses have fewer resources. Because of this, the best way to minimize risk is to use those resources in the most effective and efficient areas and to contract with professionals who will provide the highest value security.

It is important to note that time is not anybody's friend in this field. Our company recently brought on a client that spent many months deliberating with us due to slow-moving bureaucracy. While initial conversations continued, they suffered a large breach that left them with a huge mess. The fact that they could have prevented the attack was the true heartbreak. They were so close to a full team for their protection. Thankfully, we were on hand to assist with the cleanup. However, they learned the hard way: the criminals search and hope for the opportunity to find a company that will put off security, take their time with that decision and assume that a bit more time won't make a difference. Cyber liability insurance is a crucial layer of protection, and your business needs it now more than ever. Cyber liability insurance is designed to cover many of the business expenses, losses, interruption, and fines, and penalties that result from a data breach, ransomware attack, or other cyber security issues. Every business that uses any technology that connects to the Internet needs to have a policy with adequate coverage and to understand that policy fully.

Unfortunately, many business people tend to operate under the impression that their general liability insurance will cover them in the case of a cyber security issue. The truth is that most general liability insurance will not take on this huge responsibility. So, in the case of a devastating loss, these businesspeople are left with no protection because they did not verify that they were covered and take the necessary steps.

There are many possible types of losses that a business could experience as a result of a successful cyber-attack. While CLI covers many of these types of losses, just as many of them are not covered and therefore require additional endorsements. Some of the types of losses that CLI covers are:

1. *Data breaches from employee theft:*
   Disgruntled or unsavory employees are a large liability since they generally have the most direct access to your systems. This becomes more common when the employee who leaves the company harbors resentment toward their former employer.

2. *Denial-of-service attacks:*
   A denial-of-service (DoS) attack is meant to shut down a machine or network and make it inaccessible to its intended users. DoS attacks flood the targeted machine or network with traffic, such as a flood of robocalls, or sends it information that triggers a crash. In both instances, the DoS attack deprives legitimate users (i.e., employees, members, or account holders) of the intended service or resource.

3. *Cyber business interruption:*
   If your company's product or service is distributed, accessed, or managed online, a business interruption due to a cyber-attack could cause a devastating loss of sales or production.

4. *Data breaches from hacks:*
   This is another loss that is a rather broad category, as it can happen in a large number of ways and can have many outcomes and consequences. A data breach often requires a forensic audit and cleanup when the data is posted on the dark web. It takes many skillful professionals to handle a breach of this type.

It is important to remember that just because it is titled "cyber liability insurance," these policies do not magically adopt all cyber liability once you purchase. There are also many things that CLI does not cover or will only cover in particular circumstances. Many of these CLI claim denials occur because policyholders do not know or understand the exclusions and stipulations on their policy. Some of the most common reasons for denial are:

(i). *Negligence, or "failure to follow or maintain."* This is a claim denial that cites the policyholder's failure to meet and/or maintain the security standards stipulated within the policy.

(ii). *Payment card industry (PCI) fines and assessments.* Some policies contain exclusions of coverage that depend on the way the criminal(s) accessed the compromised card information, e.g., via virus or self-propagated code.

(iii). *Cyber-extortion.* It can be difficult to understand the policy clauses on extortion and ransomware. While a policy may help cover a ransom, it might not provide the coverage you need to recover from lost income.

(iv). *Social engineering.* This includes phishing and any other attack based on manipulating a user on the targeted system. Coverage for this type of loss is often not included in the main policy and will likely require an additional endorsement.

In addition to the list above, CLI also typically will not cover potential future loss of profits, loss of value due to theft of intellectual property, as well as costs to improve cyber security systems. Ensure that you thoroughly understand your policy coverages and requirements – this is the best way to easily avoid the shock of coverage denial in any of these situations.

The challenge to even qualify for a new CLI, or renew a current policy, increases every year. Businesses must follow increasingly strict security measures to be considered for coverage, whether or not a policy is already held. In the past, a business owner could simply say they implemented the correct security – now, they need to prove it. Business owners are unable to simply fill out an affidavit that they adopted and use the appropriate security measures. Many insurance providers even turn companies down and will not write the policies if the company is not up to compliance guidelines.

This is the unfortunate reality built from an increase in breaches. As companies fail to put in the preventative work, the number of breaches increases, which drives up the liability for insurance companies. This, in turn, inflates the security measures that insurance companies are forced to require to mitigate their risk. As some companies are unable to meet these strict requirements, they fall out of compliance and are left with insufficient coverage in their policies, which leaves them vulnerable. It's a cycle that continues to get more dangerous for everyone involved, and early prevention is the key to safety.

The best and most efficient way to ensure that the security standards – as well as the CLI policy itself – are understood, met, and maintained is to partner with a third-party cyber security firm. A cyber security team takes two important roles: keeping your company compliant with the CLI policy and all other relevant guidelines and conducting proactive management to minimize your risk of a breach. They will also provide validation documentation management on a continual basis to prove compliance and ensure you are eligible for coverage. It is important to note that a lot of insurance companies also have preferred vendors they use for remediation. You can have anyone you want as your cyber security team, but you may have to use someone else for the cleanup after a breach.

It takes two professional teams to ensure the safety and well-being of your company. The third-party cyber security firm is the safety – the proactive prevention specialists who will keep the risk and damage of a breach to a minimum. The cyber liability insurance is the well-being. It creates a safety net so your company can retain its health in the case that an event does happen. You must maintain both of these in order to remain fully covered.

Although it is possible for much larger companies to have an internal security officer, if you don't have a third party validate the steps you've taken to protect yourself, the insurance policy is much less likely to pay out in the case of an event. When your company experiences a breach, it is much harder to prove that it did all the right things when your security is handled internally. When a third party validates your precautions, it is much more credible. Even if the insurance policy does pay out a portion of the damages when due diligence cannot be fully proven, the premium on the policy will skyrocket.

Our firm has a client company that came on board to get assistance with compliance for their current cyber liability insurance policy, valued at $1 million. They soon accomplished this. The next year, when the policy came up for annual renewal, we were shocked to find it had more than doubled in length. In just that one year, the insurance company's security requirements, particularly for e-mail, rose to a level beyond what the client company could implement. The company could not meet the new guidelines. Consequently, the insurance company could only offer half the coverage of the previous year's policy. In our work as IT security professionals, we see this dangerous cycle continue, and we urgently tell these stories to bring to light that early preventative compliance is a team effort that can increase everyone's safety.

If you have not yet obtained crucial cyber liability insurance, here is a list of recommended steps to take:

1. Find a trusted third-party security contractor. As with many other areas in business, keep in mind that you get what you pay for. This is not an area to take shortcuts and go with the cheapest option. Remember that the key is to use your limited resources efficiently, and this is an efficient investment.
2. Have your security contractor run a full audit of your cyber security. Whether the results are good or bad, this will show you exactly where you are currently and help inform the next steps and priorities for resource allocation and timing. This

will also help the contractor learn what types of coverage you need, how much and where.

3. Receive a 'findings' report and a personalized plan of recommendations from your contracted advisors. They will advise you on what needs to be done and when.

4. Put the plan into action and stick with it. Remember that security and coverage can only work together to keep you protected if they are both maintained.

Cyber technology has created a whole new world of business. Unfortunately, as with the rest of the world, criminals will always invade and use every space available. As cybercrime rises, security regulations must follow. This is not a ploy to scam business owners into unnecessary precautions – the precautions exist because people are already being scammed every second. As long as businesses continue to operate on the web, cyber liability insurance will be absolutely essential to having a business at all.

About Scott

Scott Kreisberg founded One Step in 1985, providing technology solutions to retail businesses and helping retailers harness technology to run their businesses more efficiently. Fascinated by computers as a child, he has dedicated his entire 36-year career to the implementation and security of technology. Scott saw the role that cyber security would play in the future of retail and the critical need for improved security throughout retail businesses. His response was to form One Step Secure IT Services, a division of One Step that is designed to provide IT services and support with an emphasis on cyber security and compliance.

Knowing that a proactive and multilayered approach to cyber security was the only way businesses could truly lower their risk of a cyber-incident, Scott ensured that One Step's expertise encompassed knowledge of numerous state and industry compliance regulations. This allowed his business to provide protection not only to retail businesses but also to any business that needed to protect sensitive data and customer information. One Step Secure IT has branched out since, taking on clients in aerospace, engineering, architecture, and many other fields.

In 2004, payment card industry (PCI) compliance became a requirement for businesses, and Scott and the One Step team were quick to step in. They helped businesses navigate the requirements and ultimately worked with their clients to prevent cardholder data theft and breaches.

Businesses continue to be a prime target for cybercriminals, particularly as these businesses store increasingly massive amounts of customer data and are continually processing transactions through online networks. In more recent years, as businesses build their online presence to engage customers, the cyber security risk has skyrocketed. To mitigate this risk, Scott and the One Step team began developing partnerships with insurance companies. Scott soon realized it would now take both industries – IT security and insurance – to provide adequate protection to businesses. Now, cyber liability insurance is a critical layer of protection for any business that uses technology and stores sensitive data.

Today, One Step Secure IT – headquartered in Phoenix, Arizona, with offices in New York, Boston, and Los Angeles – is a recognized expert for many regional insurance companies to help guide businesses through policy application and recommending the correct security measures to qualify and maintain compliance for cyber liability insurance coverage. They provide education through their online blog for anyone looking to learn more about cyber security and cyber liability insurance.

You can reach Scott at:
- E-mail: SKreisberg@OneStepSecureIT.com
- LinkedIn: Scott Kreisberg (https://www.linkedin.com/in/scott-k-7463b42/)
- Website: www.OneStepSecureIT.com
- Phone: 623-227-1997

CHAPTER 12

KEEP VIRUSES AND MALWARE OFF YOUR NETWORK

BY ADAM SPENCER
Founder and CEO – 911 IT

If you get your cyber security news from popular media, you might be thinking the sky is about to fall on you and your business. Cybercrime is so widespread that it is a near certainty your business – no matter how large or how small, no matter what field you work in – will sooner or later be challenged by a cyber-attack. According to Verizon's 2019 Data Breach Investigation Report, 43% of data breaches involved small business victims, 28% of breaches involved malware, and 71% were financially motivated (see https://enterprise.verizon.com/resources/reports/2019-data-breach-investigations-report.pdf).

Here's important advice for owners and managers of small-to-medium-sized businesses: Don't waste time worrying WHETHER your IT systems will be attacked. Instead, prepare now for WHEN an attack comes. What follows are some basic facts about malware and some solid advice on how to do business safely, in spite of the threat of attack.

WHAT IS MALWARE?

Malware is a general term for any malicious software designed to harm or exploit a programmable device, service, or network. This encompasses a bunch of types and tactics: code, scripts, active content, and other software unleashed on systems like yours. They have a common purpose – to disrupt or deny your normal business operations, gather, and exploit private or proprietary information, gain unauthorized access to system resources, and steal personal or customer information as leverage to hold you and your business for ransom.

TYPES OF MALWARE

Here's a brief rundown of common malware types and the ways they can disrupt your business:

(i). *Viruses* and worms are programmed to multiply on their own, spreading across drives and networks to clog and slow system resources.

(ii). A *Trojan horse* hides itself, usually inside a legitimate application, and runs without the user knowing it's there.

(iii). *Adware* causes the computer to display pop-up messages that fool the user into clicking a link. Often installed by piggybacking with free software, adware can link to illegitimate sites, which then download spyware or ransomware to the user's network.

(iv). *Scareware* generates a pop-up with a frightening – but false – alert that your computer is compromised or has a virus. The bogus warning is intended to frighten or embarrass the victim into paying a ransom or buying software that will "release" the computer.

(v). *Spyware* sneaks onto your computer and can include a keystroke logger that captures and transmits passwords and personal or financial account information back to the hacker. The hacker can steal customer info to sell, or raid a bank account, or blackmail a user over their shady surfing habits.

(vi). *Ransomware* can lie dormant and undetected in your system while the hacker sniffs out important files. When triggered, it encrypts files in your network and cloud storage accounts, crippling the business until a ransom is paid.

(vii). *Fileless malware* uses a legitimate program to infect a computer by attacking the registry. Often it leaves behind no files, making it difficult to detect and challenging to remove.

WHAT DO HACKERS USE MALWARE FOR?

Often, cybercriminals use malware to extract or capture data so they can exert power over victims for financial gain: sometimes it's blackmail; sometimes it's theft of trade secrets, funds, or personal data; sometimes it's ransom. In today's IT economy, information is the lifeblood of business; it is often the most valuable of a company's intangible assets. A successful attack on your information systems can slow or stop your ability to pursue your business – with catastrophic consequences for your balance sheet and your business reputation.

HOW DO I KEEP MY SYSTEMS AND MY BUSINESS SAFE?

Your network is only as safe as its weakest point. Over the years, I've sometimes encountered clients who resisted adopting the security protections we recommend. This always leads to a conversation to find out where they want their security hole to be. Other clients invest in security and then want to neglect keeping their protections up-to-date. I wish it was as easy as "one and done," but you can't stop malware that was created and deployed yesterday with a security system that's months or years old. Unless you are a cyber security expert, it is so very important to get a trusted expert on your side to advise and help you install and maintain your cyber security.

The greatest strength of the Internet is also its greatest weakness. Sitting at a keyboard, anyone can access vast and valuable resources with a click of a mouse or a stroke on the keyboard. Unless you are very careful, malware can invade your systems with drastic consequences. Knowing the common points of entry can help you predict where attacks will come from.

The *Internet* has well-known sketchy websites that tempt us to visit and to click on links that infect our devices with malware. There are also impostor sites designed to mimic trusted sites; they trick us into thinking they are legitimate, so we hand over our information. It's human nature to trust, with little thought for the consequences.

Phishing via poisoned e-mail attachments. Innocent-looking attachments, including spreadsheet and word-processing files, pdfs, and zipped files, can carry malware. ***When in doubt, throw it out!***

On *social media*, people share all kinds of things, too often spreading malware without ever knowing they did it.

Items you download from the Internet or via an e-mail attachment can contain malware. A properly configured security system should block all suspicious downloads by source and type, and should scan all inbound and outbound files for malware.

An infected USB drive can compromise any device it is plugged into without the user even knowing. Leave that personal thumb drive at home and have all company devices regularly scanned for malware.

Work-from-home computers and other devices that can access your network. Even IP-connected printers can be hijacked to harbor and spread malware.

The biggest security risk is the *human factor.* We are always looking for easier ways to do things. When it comes to cyber security, however, easier is not always smarter. Using the same password on multiple accounts is easy but is definitely not as safe as creating a unique password for every account. In a perfect world, everyone in your enterprise would learn and live by security-aware best practices. In the real world, you must configure your systems and processes to enforce the levels of security you need. An expert IT partner can make this easier by setting up standards and limitations on your systems.

MULTIPLE SECURITY LAYERS WILL HELP KEEP YOUR NETWORK SAFE

Your network needs the protection of the latest cyber security tools and processes. However, these measures lose effectiveness unless they are professionally configured and maintained.

Next-Generation Antivirus (NGAV) is a new breed of software created to close gaps left by traditional antivirus software.

A properly configured *firewall* will block all unauthorized traffic to and from your network, and can detect and block malicious attempts to access the network.

Software updates and patches can catch and block new threats as they emerge. Without updates, "Zero Day" malware can exploit security flaws in popular programs before they are patched.

Ransomware detection software can detect a ransomware attack in progress and block it from continuing to run.

Zero Trust Environment is a protocol that treats every visitor and server request as a potential threat and verifies every request against approved-user credentials and permitted-process types.

Log monitoring and reporting offers real-time monitoring for errors and system changes that can detect and report an attack while it's happening. To catch an intruder before they can carry out an attack, you'll need to monitor in real time for user or permission changes.

Your systems must be backed up frequently to multiple locations. These *managed backups* reduce the amount of data that might be lost to an encryption attack. Administrators must be alerted to changes in backups beyond simple runtime reports. Your system should automatically test backups to make sure they are clean and usable to restore files.

Active *website filtering* can prevent malware from being downloaded or sent into your network and blocks outbound traffic that attempts to connect with known malicious sites.

An effective *e-mail filter* can detect and block e-mails that have malware attached.

Ongoing end-user training is crucial because 95% of cyber security breaches are caused by human error or negligence and because human actions are the #1 point of entry for viruses and malware. So, it is critical to address the human factor. You can't just tell people once and expect a change in behavior. You, or your managed services provider, must continually work with staff to inspire a culture of cyber security awareness.

Active threat hunting offers the most effective stance – you are constantly on guard, assuming at all times that your system is under attack. When an attack does happen, your security team is already on alert instead of waiting for trouble.

IT WILL HAPPEN TO YOU

Some businesspeople assume they're too small for cybercriminals to go after them. Here is what happened to the owner of a small accounting firm – let's call him John. John opened the wrong e-mail attachment – one that contained malware. The malware grabbed passwords saved in Chrome, then sent them back to the hacker. Using a stolen password to snoop through John's e-mail accounts, the hacker discovered that one of the accountant's clients was about to get a loan funded for $450,000. The hacker, posing as John, e-mailed instructions to the bank to add a payroll service to the account where the loan funds would be deposited. Hackers are smart and know how to cover their tracks. The hacker deleted each of the e-mails to and from the bank right away, even cleaning out the deleted-items folder; the accountant had no idea the messages were ever sent, received, or deleted. Neither John nor his client had any clue what was about to happen. The loan was funded on a Tuesday, and on Thursday, the $450,000 had vanished. Imagine being John, having to confess to your client that an attack on your network had caused them to lose $450,000. Talk about an awkward phone call! All this could have been avoided if the right security had been in place.

Having multilayer protections installed, tested, and properly configured provides the best chance to protect your network from viruses and malware. Hackers nowadays are smart and persistent, and sometimes can disable or bypass one of your security layers. These layers complement one another to catch invading software that may slip past one protection measure. This is why it is so important to have all the layers in place.

SEVEN QUESTIONS FOR SMALL AND MEDIUM-SIZE BUSINESS OWNERS

1. Is your network truly secured against the constant threat of attack by cybercriminals? If not, what must you do to protect yourself now?
2. Is your backup program saving ALL important data you can't afford to lose, and – more important – how quickly could you get your IT systems back to full function after a ransomware attack? Many people are shocked to discover how long this can take.
3. Are your employees using the Internet to access gambling

and porn sites, to look for jobs or shop online, or to check personal e-mail and social media? Are staff members downloading illegal music or video files, exposing you and your company to legal jeopardy? You probably assume some of this happens, but do you know how much time and risk are involved?

4. Are you certain you comply with PCI, HIPAA, CMMC, and other data-privacy laws? New regulations come into effect frequently, and it's easy to unknowingly violate them. However, if a breach occurs and an investigation reveals you didn't take necessary precautions, the bad PR and fines would still land on you. Ignorance is not an acceptable defense in a negligence lawsuit.

5. Are your firewall and antivirus tools properly configured and up-to-date? "Set and forget" is not a safe policy when it comes to firewall protection. It must be constantly monitored and conscientiously updated – is yours?

6. Are your employees storing confidential or private information using unprotected cloud apps like Dropbox that are OUTSIDE your backup program? Could they quit their job with a list of all your clients and go to work for a competitor?

And finally, this is the most important question of all:

7. As a business owner, are you too busy managing the work you already do to become a cyber security expert? If you don't have plenty of time to keep current with the latest threats and defenses, and plenty of expertise to combat them, consider signing up with a managed services provider whose reputation depends on protecting businesses like yours from the constantly evolving threat of hacking, malware, and virus attacks.

About Adam

Adam Spencer is the founder and CEO of 911 IT, a highly-regarded, managed IT services provider in Salt Lake City, Utah. Adam began his IT career right out of high school, working as a computer repair technician for a local Internet service provider. When the ISP went out of business, Adam started his own IT support company to help pay for his studies at Utah Valley University. He soon discovered that his love for the work – and the money he was earning – surpassed what his studies in school could provide.

Adam founded 911 IT in 2004, with the goal of helping people and businesses meet the most common and the most complex computer repair and network management challenges. As the security and privacy aspects of IT have expanded and grown more sophisticated, so has the company's menu of services.

What has not changed is Adam's love for his profession and his dedication to his clients. He says, "Why do I do it? I love IT and all the challenges that come with it. Every day I get to collaborate with companies to help them reach and exceed their business goals through IT. It brings me joy to teach others how technology can simplify their work, helping them achieve more in business with less effort. I have helped many companies grow faster and more easily than they had ever thought possible by helping them integrate more useful technology into their business operations."

911 IT serves a wide range of clients, with a growing clientele in the financial and health care sectors, helping to manage and advance the stringent security and privacy standards in those industries. The 911 IT client roster includes small and medium-sized companies in such industries as financial, health care, spas, transportation, construction, manufacturing, and more.

From expert cloud and backup services, data security and privacy compliance, to affordable 24/7 network uptime monitoring and response, 911 IT provides custom-configured service to thousands of companies and individuals, meeting all their requirements for IT Support, server administration, and cyber security. For example, the *911 IT Worry Free* IT package covers everything needed to assure clients that their network is secure, and their customers' vital data is safe.

Proud to offer a combination of traditional business integrity and cutting-edge IT best practices, Adam makes this pledge:

- *We answer our phones live*
- *We do what's right even when it's not profitable for us*
- *We are proud of the work we do and back our performance with a 100% satisfaction guarantee*
- *We believe that your success is ours, and that's why we always go the extra mile*

As the IT industry continues to evolve, Adam Spencer vows that 911 IT will always work to be a trusted partner to all customers, both new and long-established.

Contact

Adam Spencer, CEO/Founder
911 IT | IT Services & Support for Salt Lake City
1124 South Jordan Parkway
South Jordan, UT 84118

- E-mail: adam@911it.com
- LinkedIn: https://www.linkedin.com/in/adam-spencer-61826140/
- Facebook: https://www.facebook.com/911ITService/
- Blog: https://www.911it.com/category/blog/
- Web: https://www.911it.com/
- Phone: 801-610-6000

CHAPTER 13

OUTSMARTING US WITH SOCIAL ENGINEERING

BY ALVION "AL" LEGALL
Founder and CEO – ABL Computers

We're all familiar with the scene: a shadowy room, dark save for the glow of various screens. Some feature surveillance footage; others show lines upon lines of code – indecipherable to the average reader. A hunched and foreboding figure sits in front of the monitors, watching and typing rapidly. Here sits the ominous hacker...or, at least, the version of a hacker we've come to expect out of films and TV shows.

Thanks to Hollywood's dramatization of the pastime, hackers carry an otherworldly aura about them – geniuses, they wear hooded sweatshirts and focus their time and energy breaking into whatever high-stakes mainframe they've been hired to crack. Because of this archetype, many people believe that hacking itself is difficult, that it's this highly technical thing that only the most elite programmers can do.

This is a common and dangerous misconception. Hacking isn't hard, and it's not even that technical. The truth is, it's almost entirely psychological, and anyone can do it simply by being observant.

A while back, I was doing a demonstration. As an exercise, I asked someone in the group to go online and find a video of a crying baby. Then I asked a woman in the crowd to call a cable company, posing as someone's wife.

The story I asked the woman to give was simple: she was at home, but her husband wasn't. She wasn't the owner of their cable account, but their daughter wanted to watch some shows. She pleaded with them to just allow her to add the children's package to their account. I told her to act stressed-out, overwhelmed, and tired.

This request would have been against the company's regulations because the husband wasn't present, and it was his name, not hers, on their hypothetical account. She didn't have the authorization to add the package. As the representative on the phone tried to explain this, I had my audience member play the audio of the baby crying in the background. The woman pretended to become stressed out and the representative gave in. They broke regulations and added the children's package.

I had no way of actually knowing this would work. I didn't know the representative, and I hadn't staged anything about the exercise beyond what my audience witnessed. The reason it worked is simple – the sound of a baby, combined with a stressed mother, creates empathy. The representative felt sorry for her.

We hacked the cable company... and it worked.

This is the thing people need to realize about social engineering. At its core, it's about getting to know you. It's a digital con, and it can often happen right under your nose without you realizing it for months.

Many of us are aware that our data is being shared to some extent. In this day and age, it's taken for granted that people are out there lurking, that the wrong stroke of bad luck could mean our credit card numbers being compromised.

So, we protect ourselves. We create passwords and PINs, and we cross our fingers, hoping the next person who gets "hacked" won't be us. And some of that stuff works. It helps to create security questions, provided you don't answer one of those Facebook surveys essentially broadcasting their answers. It helps to have PIN numbers and passwords and to set your social media accounts to "private."

Until it doesn't.

Hackers are observant. They get to know your habits, your lifestyles, your preferences, where you shop, what you collect, even what your favorite ice cream flavor is. It might seem like it doesn't matter that you love 'rum raisin'. But then, one day you might complain publicly that you love shopping at one particular grocery store, but they don't carry your favorite brand.

If a hacker is watching – and they generally are – all they would have to do is craft a believable-looking ad for that grocery store advertising that they finally carry that particular 'rum raisin' ice cream. Then they will send that ad to your e-mail address with a pretty good bet that you'll click on it.

When you click on links you're not sure of; you run the risk of accidentally downloading a whole slew of malware. One popular technique for hackers is to use ransomware to steal your information and then hold it for ransom. They will demand a certain sum in return for the stolen information, whether it's important files or credit card numbers, access to programs you need for work, etc.

In the movies, we seem to only ever hear the word "ransom" when this type of thing is being done to someone famous, maybe a politician or the CEO of a big corporation. The ransom money is always an extravagant amount, and as viewers, we detach ourselves from the scenario because of it. Most of us don't have millions of dollars in the bank that could be ransomed, so we've learned to assume that hackers looking for a payout are only looking for large sums.

The truth is that hackers usually leave those people alone because they're more likely to warrant a federal investigation. Large sums of money get attention. They know that smaller individuals will not trigger government intervention the way a larger company or high roller might. So, instead, they go for the low-hanging fruit.

They target smaller amounts from everyday people. They'll use social engineering to determine how much you can probably afford to spend on a ransom. You may not be able to afford tens of thousands of dollars, but you might be able to afford a thousand. So, the hacker will steal your data and demand $800. Because that's realistic in your budget, you'll likely pay it to get your stuff back.

So, how do they determine what that budget is? That data is basically given to them.

Banks and credit card companies have access to all your financial records. They know how and where you spend your money, and they share that data with larger companies like Target, Walmart, etc.

These companies benefit from this information because they are all competing to get your business. Hackers will use this information to get to know you. They'll get a feel for your finances so they can figure out what your budget is before they ever ask for the amount.

What hackers are truly good at is social engineering, and as a society, we make it easy for them to access the information they need. Benjamin Franklin once said, "They who can give up essential liberty to obtain a little temporary safety deserve neither liberty nor safety."

In an ironic sense, this rings true to this day, and it can be applied to the public's affinity for social media. Hackers don't need to find out your social security number. All they need to know are the answers to your security *questions*. Whether it's a chain-letter-styled survey shared over and over, asking questions about their first pet, their favorite color, or their mother's maiden name, people share their information online all the time and hardly give it any thought.

It doesn't stop with surveys either. Social media is an environment where people are encouraged to tell others about their day, their personal life, and how they're feeling. They share pictures of everything they do and even announce to the world *where* they're doing it. Online, people post photos of themselves on vacation, they tag where they are every Memorial Day, they post where their children attend school and what neighborhood block party they plan to attend.

And remember, hackers meet people on an emotional level more than anything. By accepting friend requests from people you don't know – or a duplicated account from someone you do know – you're inviting them into your digital home. Once they're in, they'll start crafting a relationship in some way. They could be there for months studying everything you're doing, figuring out how you behave and what you spend money on.

Then there are the sneakier, professional methods of social engineering – the sanctioned companies that essentially purchase access to our lives. People don't often stop to think about *why* services like Facebook are available for free; they are seemingly limitless databases providing constant connection to however many friends and family members all the time, yet everyone knows that these companies are multibillion-dollar enterprises.

So, what does Facebook sell? Facebook sells *you*. You are the product that is sold to companies, or, more specifically, your *attention* is the product. Software engineers are paid hundreds of thousands of dollars a year to code algorithms designed to catalog your interests and send ads and posts that pertain to those passions. If you love turtles, they'll send you turtles. If you love traveling, you'll get ads about airfare.

Hackers use this information in a similar way. They'll watch you for months, learning what you're interested in and what kinds of ads you tend to click on. Then, when they've learned enough, they'll strike, sending predatory e-mails with links that result in ransomware downloads or compromised passcodes.

Or, sometimes, they'll call you. They'll tell you there is an urgent matter that you must attend to. They will make it seem like a life-or-death situation, or they'll tell you that if you don't cooperate, there will be some sort of legal repercussion. Rest assured, if federal agencies want to arrest you, they will come and break down your doors. They certainly aren't going to call you and let you know first.

I try to educate my clients about this whenever I can. There is never anything that is so urgent that it must be dealt with right away. Stop and think for just a moment before responding. It's never life-or-death.

Hackers calling and posing as representatives of a federal agency or a collection service is one of the most common ways that people have their identities stolen. They prey on the empathy and fear of others and, once they have access to whatever information they need, the damage has been done. You could have all the documentation and answers to security questions that can prove who you are, but if a hacker has that information too, it does you very little good.

This is why it's so hard to recover from identity theft, and most organizations are not sympathetic to that sort of thing. Generally, if you are the victim of identity theft, you'll still have to pay the debt, even if it's not your fault.

I was recently able to avoid a scenario where I myself nearly fell victim to a hacking scheme. I received an e-mail about one of my credit cards. That e-mail asked that I click on a link to update some information regarding the card account. I happened to remember that I don't generally use that particular e-mail address for banking, so while they were sending the e-mail to an address they'd linked to me, they hadn't realized the distinction.

If I hadn't taken a moment to think about it, I might have clicked that malicious link, believing it to be legitimate. I took an extra second to consider where I normally get my banking information sent, so I was able to avoid an attack and prevented my data from being stolen by a hacker.

Hackers also like using scare tactics by pretending to be government entities, like the IRS, because people immediately panic. The hacker might say you haven't paid a tax, and they've been trying to reach you. In these cases, you should never give them any payment information. Rest assured, if the IRS wants to contact you, they're not going to call you on the phone. To handle things like this properly, ask that they send you the bill in the mail instead. Then you'll be able to look up the receipt number on the IRS website to verify its legitimacy.

The thing is, we live in a world of convenience. A lot of us will risk everything just to make things simpler for ourselves. As a society, we crave the quick and easy fix: *Don't bother me. I'll pay online. I'll opt for automatic payments for my subscriptions.* Many of us are so inundated with stressors and details in our professional and personal lives that any shortcut we can use feels like a relief. We prefer the path of least resistance, and hackers hedge their bets on that exact characteristic.

By taking the extra steps to double-check your privacy settings, look up receipt numbers, use multiple fingers when you type your passcode into an ATM or debit machine, and double-check an e-mail address, you may take an extra second to accomplish basic tasks, but you'll also make it harder for someone to steal your identity or your data.

About Alvion

Alvion Legall is the founder and CEO of ABL Computers. He grew up in the island country of Trinidad and Tobago at the southernmost part of the Caribbean chain near South America. Although his first interaction with computers didn't happen until he was in college, he became immediately enamored with them. By the end of his first semester, he'd become so knowledgeable that he was offered a job by the technology department as an adjunct professor.

During the school year, he would learn new programs, and then, in the summers, he would teach professors how to use those programs. Then, in the fall, he would sit as a student in their classes. He continued to do this for nearly four years, working his way through school by teaching.

By the time he graduated in 2001, Alvion knew he wanted to work in technology full-time. He took a leap of faith and launched his own business, ABL Computers, pulling from the skills and experiences he'd garnered as an adjunct.

What began as a humble and very specific service gradually developed into a fully functioning enterprise offering advanced security and IT services to clients throughout New York. Today, ABL Computers provides reliable IT services, focusing mainly on financial investment firms and medical offices, where top-of-the-line security is critical. Alvion concentrates on crisis prevention, ensuring that virus outbreaks, security issues, and other technical problems are kept to a minimum so that employees can perform their best.

Alvion's perspective has always been that an educated customer is his best client. As with his professors years ago, he educates his clients to make sure they can comfortably make informed decisions to benefit their businesses.

One particular way Alvion seeks to better educate his clients is by teaching about social engineering and how various sites, social media platforms, and other organizations utilize your data in tricky, often predatory ways. He believes this particular form of education is one of the key components of cyber security, as informed decision-making for every business owner, employee, and even student is the first line of defense against potentially disastrous outcomes.

When he's not working, Alvion enjoys spending time with his wife, Maxine, and their two daughters. His children both share a love of music, and Alvion provides audio-technical help at their singing engagements. When he's not working in technology, he spends time in the kitchen, expanding his culinary skills with new foods whenever he can. He and his wife love entertaining guests at their home and providing a close-knit family life for their children. They are also passionate about providing opportunities to others and work with their local church to donate laptops to students in need who are going off to college for the first time.

You can reach Alvion at:
- E-mail: Alvion@ablcomputers.com
- LinkedIn: https://www.linkedin.com/in/alvion-legall-9bb34230
- Web: https://www.ablcomputers.com
- Phone: 718-848-8102

CHAPTER 14

HOW YOUR EMPLOYEES UNINTENTIONALLY OPEN THE DOOR FOR HACKERS

BY JOSEPH SALAZAR
Vice President (Ops.) – Netwiz Computers

The Internet has revolutionized communications across the world like nothing before. It allows people and organizations the opportunity to have countless interactions across the globe. The Internet's worldwide broadcasting capabilities are unprecedented. Geographic location is no longer a factor when it comes to information dissemination and collaboration between individuals and their computers.

We have come to rely on the Internet for many things, from communication to networking to research and to a thousand other business-related activities. But the more we use it, the more attractive it is to cybercriminals. They search the web to gather sensitive information, especially personal and financial information, in order to commit identity theft, fraud, and other crimes.

Nearly every company today is connected to the Internet – employees' computers are networked to the Internet, so everyone relies on this infrastructure to communicate and perform normal business operations. IT departments typically have a defense set up to protect against unwanted online activity. Some methods include installing a firewall, blocking access to unwanted websites, and making sure every computer has antivirus software and that it stays up to date. Ironically, it is not your hardware or software that makes your company most vulnerable to cybercrime – it is your employees.

Employee activity is the most dangerous threat to any network. And most of the time, they are not even aware of the damage they are causing. Often, it is as simple as a click on an unknowingly suspicious e-mail link, a visit to a wrong web page, or even the use of an infected USB drive. Any of these can occur on a regular workday, and, within seconds your network is compromised.

That is why it is imperative to train every employee, every subcontractor, and any individual accessing your network data in the latest practices and procedures for cybersecurity. This training must be an ongoing effort by everyone. An annual class on how to avoid e-mail scams and not download random attachments is not good enough. The business world is connected constantly, so cybercriminals have more opportunities to take advantage of individuals and businesses today than they did 20 years ago. So, in response to a more constant threat, companies must remain vigilant by consistently training their employees to better protect themselves and the company.

In addition to consistent cybersecurity training, it is also smart to send out weekly e-mails to employees that inform them what threats they should be aware of and how to identify a breach should it occur. Their training should also teach them a plan of action for those times when a breach does occur. It is crucial that employees are constantly aware of threats they may encounter and what they should do if they mistakenly allow a breach. The natural response for most employees, when they've allowed a breach, is to stick their head in the sand as if nothing happened and hope that it goes away somehow. They hope IT will not know they were the cause of the breach. They may feel their job is on the line and that alerting network administrators may put their job at risk. Therefore, consistent training and communication are needed – *you must recondition your employees' natural response.*

We at Netwiz use several excellent third-party tools that assist us in ensuring that our employees are well-trained and that they are rewarded when they identify an incident. For example, our workers go through a Comprehensive Cybersecurity Training Class where they read and sign guidelines for Company Best Network Computing Practices. We communicate consistently by sending out weekly e-mails that detail various breaches and provide tactics to help them spot something similar and report it.

Biweekly e-mails are sent out as tests by recreating samples of phishing e-mails, SMS messages, and Facebook messaging. With people connected to so many different forms of communication, it is imperative that they see the variety of threats that exist. These e-mails go out to everyone in the company on different days and in different formats. This way, we can see who clicks on what links and who does not. Employees who fail these biweekly e-mail tests by falling for the attack are asked to repeat the cybersecurity class, and if any employee opens six of the phishing test e-mails within a six-month period, they can be subjected to disciplinary action.

While e-mails are the most common choice used by cybercriminals, infected USB drives are another point of entry companies must guard against. All USB drives must stay on-site and must be cleaned by a dedicated computer to ensure the drives are clean prior to using them on any computer system. Outside USB drives, or ones that employees bring from home, are the most dangerous to a network because the network administrators for your company are not managing computers that are outside your network. Therefore, they cannot make sure the proper antivirus and cybersecurity plans are installed. This rule about no outside USB drives also applies to any USB cable, especially the ones people use to charge their mobile devices. These should never be plugged into company computers. Your company should have a policy in place that prevents this from happening and should provide secure and approved power plugs and cables to employees who need to charge their phones. They must also always be plugged into a power strip or a wall socket.

Network administrators do not have the capacity to manage all personal handheld devices, so they must make sure those are powered by a power circuit. One reason no outside USB cables should be allowed is because cybercriminals use something called a Ninja Cable. A USB Ninja Cable is a regular-looking USB cable designed to infect any device it is connected to with malware. Once this malicious cable is plugged into a USB-friendly device, it injects keystrokes onto your computer that allows the attacker to gain remote access to your private files by downloading malware and infecting your device. A USB Ninja Cable can be configured to carry many forms of malware. Ransomware is often used, where the bad actor gains access to your computer files, holding them for ransom until you pay to have them released.

What does a Ninja Cable look like? That is what makes this type of attack so scary – *you cannot tell a Ninja Cable apart from an ordinary USB cable.* They look the same and feel the same in your hand. They even function the same way too. The Ninja Cable will charge your phone just like a normal USB cable, which makes it so difficult to know which cord is problematic. Once a Ninja Cable is connected to your computer, it waits until your device is idle for a set period of time, such as five minutes. Then, the injected keystrokes that infect your computer with malware can be set to activate. This keystroke injection runs quickly and is easy to miss, which is why this type of attack is super-effective and almost undetectable. The best way to avoid this situation is to only buy USB cables and jump drives from reputable stores and never use a random USB cable that has not been approved by your network administrator.

Since every employee needs access to your network to perform basic business operations, it is important their passwords are strong enough to do their job properly. Passwords are the first line of defense for protecting network information, whether it is personal, business, or financial. A weak password is a simple password – one that may just be a word. For example, never use "password" as your password for a device. It makes it too easy for cybercriminals to figure it out. It is like leaving the doors to your house open. A strong password is one that has a complex configuration, no fewer than eight characters in length and including a combination of upper- and lower-case letters along with numbers and symbols. One method is to choose a word and consistently replace letters in it with symbols or numbers. For example, if your original password is "LosAngeles," you can make it stronger by substituting some letters with numbers and symbols. So, it could be converted to "L0sAng3l3@)@!" where the "o" is changed to "0," the "e" is changed to "3," and the last four characters are the year "2021" by holding the shift key while keying in those numbers, which gives you symbols.

Social engineering is a popular tactic bad actors use to gain access to your company's network and files. It is natural that good people want to help others. Unfortunately, cybercriminals take advantage of this fact. Our natural inclination to help others explains why social engineering has become such a powerful tool in the hands of fraud artists. Where a strong password prevents criminals from hacking systems, and a security system prevents them from breaking into a workplace, social engineers circumvent these security measures by tricking people into simply handing over the information they want, often by impersonating someone over the phone or sending deceptive e-mail messages. Since there is no technological defense against this kind of attack, your employees need to be on their guard.

For example, a woman walks into an office, using social engineering to gain control of a company's network. She approaches the receptionist at the front desk, saying she has an interview in a little bit but that she has a problem. She just spilled coffee on her résumé and does not have time to run home and print another copy prior to her meeting. During this conversation, the social engineer builds a rapport with the receptionist. Maybe she notices a picture of a cat on the desk, and she mentions her love of cats and how she has three at home. She hands the receptionist a jump drive and asks if she would please print out a new copy of her résumé since hers has coffee stains on it. Since the receptionist believes she is helping someone in need, she inserts the unapproved USB device into her company computer and grants it access to the network. The jump drive has two résumé files on it, so the receptionist clicks on both files, but only one opens a résumé. The other file is not a résumé at all. Even though it resembles a Word document, it is ransomware that the receptionist unknowingly just uploaded to the company network. The only person who knows what just happened is the cybercriminal who tricked the receptionist into uploading her virus onto the company's network. So now the bad actors have control of that network and all the files it contains – all because the receptionist thought she was helping someone in need.

Here are other examples of how employees can wreak havoc on a company's cybersecurity:

- A former employee with admin rights holds the network hostage by refusing to give up passwords
- A network engineer becomes aware he is about to be fired, so he resets the hardware to factory defaults
- A payroll company employee files fraudulent tax returns by using data she has access to
- Someone working at the Department of Human Assistance Benefits in California steals information and has fraudulent welfare checks sent to friends and family
- A cybercriminal posing as someone from IT calls an employee, claiming they need their login and password information to run a software update

Given all these examples, you may be wondering how to protect yourself and how to protect your company from cybercriminals. Stay vigilant, stay aware and stay educated, so you understand the risks and adopt best practices in information security.

This chapter has discussed various ways that employees become the weakest link in cybersecurity, while offering suggestions on how to improve the human element of your company's network security. It is widely known that a username and password must be strong to combat cybercrime, but each employee also plays an important role in keeping a network secure. Each one is a gatekeeper and must be trained to understand the weight of that responsibility.

About Joseph

Joseph Salazar is the Vice President of Operations at Netwiz Computers, located in Placentia, California. He lives nearby in Yorba Linda and has nearly 30 years of experience working in the IT industry. Starting out as a help-desk IT support technician, Joseph quickly climbed the ranks, gaining industry knowledge with every step he took, leading him to where he is today.

Joseph got into this field because he was fascinated by how important problem-solving was in the IT industry, and he noticed how solutions were constantly having to adapt to new threats. When several IT firms were hit with ransomware, he spent weeks working intensely with these firms, figuring out how they had been attacked and what they could do to ensure it didn't happen to his clients. He quickly realized it was important not just to find out what caused a cyberattack but also to figure out how to prevent it from happening in the future. Each day brought a new threat, and each day he brought a new solution.

In addition to his role at Netwiz Computers, Joseph also takes pride in being active in his community. He is the president of the Brea Kiwanis Club, serving a third term. They do various fundraisers that help less fortunate kids in the area. One fundraiser is a Back-to-School Event, where they take 80 underprivileged kids to JCPenney and buy them $100 worth of clothes, so they have something to wear to school. His Kiwanis Club also puts on a popular citywide spelling bee. In an effort to help out with higher education costs, they give out over $10,000 in college grants every year. Joseph is also an active member of the Brea and Yorba Linda Chambers of Commerce, where he enjoys attending their events throughout the year.

As Vice President of Operations for Netwiz Computers, Joseph helps his company serve the Orange County area by providing reliable, consistent, and professional IT services. They have been successful at doing this since 1998. They focus on providing their clients with enterprise-level services and solutions for small businesses. Time and experience have helped them develop best practices and workflow procedures around a proactive philosophy designed to minimize disruption and keep their clients focused on their business, not their technology.

You can connect with Joseph at:
- E-mail: joe@netwizcomputers.com
- Web: NetwizComputers.com
- Phone: 714-455-2925

CHAPTER 15

KEEPING OUR CHILDREN SAFE ONLINE

BY JULIO LOPEZ
Founder & CEO
– IT for Education: A Division of Net A Corp

The first sound a child hears in the morning may be a smartphone alarm, and the last thing they might see before falling asleep is a TikTok video. In between, they may log onto tablets or computers for lessons and homework and return to the screen later to game with friends, video chat with grandparents, or stream a movie.

The internet has become an integral part of children's lives, as they rely on it for learning, socializing, play, and entertainment. It's given them a way to maintain a sense of normalcy while social distancing and countless other benefits. However, the amount of time kids spend connected to digital devices makes it nearly impossible for adults to monitor their online behaviors to ensure they are safe.

This job was a lot easier for parents twenty years ago, when those fortunate enough to have a family computer could require kids to ask permission for a turn, so they knew when each child was using it and for how long. The desktop was usually kept in a common room, with the monitor in plain sight, so a parent would know if their child was reading articles for a social studies paper, playing the Sims, or entering an unsavory chat room.

Today's ever-shrinking screen sizes make it difficult to keep an eye on kids' online activities. Even if sitting next to one another on the couch, a parent may not be able to see what a child is doing on their smartphone. And worse, device portability and ubiquitous Wi-Fi make digital environments more accessible so kids can browse and log onto portals from places where supervision is not feasible, such as the bus or playground.

If we thought a glowing screen accompanied an excessive amount of children's experiences before, enter the COVID-19 Pandemic. When students went from in-classroom learning to an exclusively online environment overnight, these tiny machines became their entire universe.

ADVANTAGES OF THE INTERNET FOR LEARNING

The internet has proven to be an incredible tool for learning. Since vast amounts of information can be accessed with a few key words in a search engine, students can create well-researched projects, not to mention they can choose specific topics that hold their interest. At young ages, kids can also develop skills in areas such as culinary arts, crafts, sports, dance, or home repair by watching tutorials or reading blogs.

While digital natives get a bad rap for weak verbal communication skills, the internet actually increases opportunities to network and talk with others beyond school and cultural boundaries. Internet access can also even the playing field, bringing an expansive view of the world to those with otherwise limited resources.

Interactive tools and the variety of digital content types can accommodate students' sensory-based learning styles to help them gather and process information. Assignment checklists, images, and videos support visual learners, recorded stories or even the instructor's voice appeal to auditory processors, and chat capabilities keep social learners engaged.[1]

RISKS AND PROTECTIONS

In order to be better prepared to protect our children, we must be aware of the internet's technological, physical, and psychological risks. The increase in screen time caused by remote learning means kids are even more vulnerable than ever to threats like cyberbullying, inappropriate content, predators, scams, phishing, and ransomware attacks.

We will cover two main areas that you'll need to understand to keep your kids safe online. First, we'll address technological considerations—the first mode of defense. We'll provide guidelines for how schools, parents, and students can work together to safeguard systems against cyberattacks.

Next, we'll approach the human element. As both an IT professional and a father, I'm passionate about harnessing the power of education and communication to protect children from dangers that can harm them emotionally.

Let's Talk Tech...

It's second nature for adults to do everything possible to keep our families, homes, finances, and computers secure, but kids who have their basic needs met do not tend to worry about safety. This makes it our responsibility to ensure kids can critically interpret information and protect themselves when surfing the web and consuming media. Educators—from classroom teachers to technology coaches and school administrators—should lead the ever-evolving digital literacy conversation with both kids and parents.

---

1. Driver, Helen. (2020, January 18) Developing Online Courses For All Learning Styles. *eLearning Industry.* https://elearningindustry.com/ developing-online-courses-for-different-learning-styles

INTERNET SAFETY

Children and adults alike can and should be taught the basic tenets of safe internet practices.

1. Only visit safe websites

It is becoming increasingly difficult to tell the difference between a "safe" website and a risky one, but I have two recommendations. One, check the URL before you click on it. Make sure it starts with **https**. The "s" stands for "secure." If there isn't an "s" – don't trust the site. A second indicator that a site is safe is the presence of a lock symbol to the left of the URL in the address bar.

2. Only access secure networks

It's important to teach our children to only use networks that are secure. Free Wi-Fi network connections, for one, cannot always be trusted. If possible, use your own device's hotspot because it is likely encrypted. If you do connect to a public Wi-Fi network, do not access personal or financial information or stay logged into a site for a long time.[2]

3. Follow password safety protocols

All users should be taught and encouraged to create and memorize strong, unique passwords. This practice helps to safeguard the systems you access and the valuable information they house.

Many people make the mistake of using the same password for all portals and apps. If you reuse a password over and over again, all it takes is one instance of being cracked to completely expose all of your accounts to innumerable threats. Create a separate password for each login.

Two basic tips for creating strong passwords:

---

2. Federal Trade Commission. (2021, May). How To Safely Use Public Wi-Fi Networks. https://www.consumer.ftc.gov/articles/how-safely-use-public-wi-fi-networks

- Don't use a single word such as **password** or a commonly used phrase like **Iloveyou.**
- Don't include information about your life that is easy to find out, such as the names and birthdays of your loved ones, favorite music artists and sports teams, or expressions you often say.

Too frequently, I see people make the major mistake of writing down their password on a piece of paper then sliding it under their keyboard, or worse: posting it on the monitor. This is an invitation for others to access the network or other resources, making the password useless.

4. Take precautions against cyberattacks

Minimize exposure to ransomware and other malicious attacks by following these actions. Read other chapters in this book for more extensive explanations and tips.

(i). Regularly update devices with important patches and use preventative software.
(ii). When using email, verify senders, and use extra caution before clicking on a link or viewing an attachment.
(iii). Enable Multi-Factor Authentication whenever possible.
(iv). Keep informed about cybersecurity threats and ransomware techniques.

KIDS' SAFETY AND WELLBEING

From the moment they're born, children are exposed to technology. As babies, they hold their parents' cell phones and watch colorful cartoons. By the time they're three-to-four years old, they may have tablets of their own. These devices have essentially become digital babysitters, as parents leave toddlers alone with them when they take a work call, do the dishes, or simply need a break. These very young children may benefit from developing intuition about technology, but they are also exposed to its dangers earlier than ever.

(I). Predators

When we talk about keeping children safe online, most people immediately associate the topic with predators. That's because stories about the dangers of strange adults messaging children are frequently picked up by news outlets, so they get a lot of noise.

Unfortunately, this glaring issue isn't simply hype, and parents—you're not going to like the reason, but you need to hear this. One of the biggest safety hazards is social media behavior—yours. When you tag your child in photos on social media, you provide their name and what they look like. And if you geotag your kid at school, you are telling adults which institution they attend, providing a roadmap that leads directly to them.

If we're going to teach kids how to stay safe online, we have to lead by example. Social media can be a fun way to stay connected with people, but we have to use it responsibly.

Familiarize yourself with your kids' social media pages and monitor their posts. This way, you can help them detect strange interactions before they put themselves at risk. It will annoy them and generate eye-rolls, but it is imperative to know who your kids are talking to at all times.

Adults have the ability to be discerning and know people aren't always who they say they are. Most children don't have life experiences that make them question credibility, though. Predatory adults take advantage of this and use the barrier of a screen to pretend to be anyone they want, including another kid. It's up to us to teach children to be cautious and how to avoid dangerous situations.

Body safety cannot be emphasized enough, both in the

physical world and online. Encourage bodily autonomy and establishing proper boundaries. Saying "no" to uncomfortable, inappropriate, or dangerous situations could save your child's life.

It's also important to review the apps and sites your kids access. You may put device restrictions in place that require parental permission to download apps, but unless you take the time to check out each app that your child wants to acquire, this safety measure is ineffective. Too often, parents blindly approve a download without looking at the content and features to make sure it looks legit and safe.

Follow safe search practices. Choose search engines such as Safe Search Kids or Kidz-search for younger kids. If using Google, we suggest you activate "safe search" settings.

(II). Set up ground rules

You wouldn't hand your car keys to a 16-year-old without giving them driving lessons, making sure they've earned a license, then establishing rules. The same parental controls should apply to technology use.

Kids need to be equally informed about safety and risks before they go online. Tell them to avoid sharing personal information, photos, or videos on public forums or with people they don't know. Establish clear guidelines to give your children their best chance at staying safe.

Foster an environment of trust between you and your child. They need to feel safe to come to you or another trusted adult if someone online asks them to engage in inappropriate behavior such as meeting in person.[3]

---

3. Immediately report alarming behavior, especially child exploitation to the police, FBI (https://tips.fbi.gov) or the National Center for Missing & Exploited Children (1-800-843-5678 or report.cybertip.org).

Minimize their exposure by limiting recreational time online. Allow kids to instant message friends, play games, and participate in social media, but regulate the duration and perhaps designate small periods of time for it right after school.

In cases where there are older siblings in the house, talk to them about their online activities and find out what they show to younger children. Encourage them to be responsible and help keep their younger siblings safe.

We understand that for logistical purposes, a lot of parents set their kids up with computers in their bedrooms, but if that device were centrally located instead, you could keep an eye on things like it's 1999. If adults or older siblings are nearby, kids are also less likely to talk to sketchy people or visit inappropriate sites.

Another safeguard to look into is basic web filters that allow kids to access age-appropriate content. Some internet service providers often include them, along with further guidance and resources.

(III). Monitor The Emotional Strain of Living Online

These silent killers are the psychological and emotional results of a fully digitized world. Learn more to be able to defend your children from these dangers that constantly hold our children under siege.

(IV). Cyberbullying

Another danger that has gotten a lot of press in recent years is cyberbullying, and rightfully so. Children are regularly bullied online—in front of the whole world—by both peers and perfect strangers. The internet exposes them to some of the most mentally and verbally abusive aspects of society.

Keep an eye out for any cyberbullying, as it can have

serious mental and emotional consequences. Pay attention to changes in your child's behavior, including increased anxiety, signs of depression, and any attempts at hiding online activity.

(V). Avoid Social Isolation
Kids are becoming less and less comfortable with in-person socialization. Many children would rather play games on their tablet than kick a ball, climb trees, or play dress-up with friends. Lack of social interaction inhibits soft skill development, nurtures social anxieties, and ultimately damages the ability to form and build relationships. This affected us all to some degree when we were denied the option of socializing due to social distancing requirements during the COVID-19 Pandemic. Many children faced the stressors of instant isolation at a pinnacle point in their development.

THE ILLUSION OF SOCIAL MEDIA

It's no secret that there is a huge difference between reality and the way people present their lives online. Adults and children alike know better, but still, we fall for the false narrative that everyone else looks and lives better than us. This belief has a serious negative impact on our mental health.

Plastic surgeons have actually coined a new disorder called Snapchat Dysmorphia to describe an alarming number of adults asking to be altered to resemble Snapchat filters in real life. The popularity of editing our appearance and the platforms that make it possible has a devastating effect on kids' self-esteem. Parents need to work to build their children's confidence and openly discuss the boundary between digital image manipulation and reality. If your child shows signs of any type of dysmorphia, they should be treated by a professional.[4]

4. Muacevic, Alexander. Adler, John R. (2018, March). Is "Snapchat Dysmorphia" a Real Issue? *Cureus.* https://www.ncbi.nlm.nih.gov/pmc/articles/ PMC5933578/

EDUCATE EVERYONE

One of the biggest problems facing our children is that not everybody knows about the threats. Adults tend to keep kids in the dark, in part because they underestimate their capacity to grasp the issues.

This avoidance is highly problematic, as many kids are not only in vulnerable spaces but are quite tech-savvy. Consider, for a moment, that children as young as nine are beginning to display hacker-level computer proficiency. Educating kids as early as possible with age-appropriate material cultivates a grassroots understanding of the dangers as well as protective measures.

As technology advances and evolves, so will the risks. The key is to stay alert, constantly educate yourself, and implement safety guidelines for both school and home to help protect children when they browse, learn, and socialize online.

Helpful Resources

Common Sense
Media and technology safety resources for parents, educators, and advocates
https://commonsense.org

National CyberSecurity Alliance: A Teacher's Guide To Student Online
Safety https://staysafeonline.org/blog/teachers-guide-student-online-safety/

N.B. Immediately report alarming behavior, especially child exploitation, to the police, FBI
(https://tips.fbi.gov), or the National Center for Missing & Exploited Children
(1-800-843-5678 or report.cybertip.org). (Repeated from footnote#3)

About Julio

Julio Lopez is the Founder of IT for Education: A Division of Net A Corp. Julio serves as its CEO and is able to share knowledge and serve others. The company has been committed to its mission to empower K–12 educators and students through technology since its inception in 2002.

Julio's team of systems engineers brings decades of combined experience serving schools, administrators, faculty, and students. Their broad background includes technology architecture, systems integration, infrastructure design, and IT security.

The company specializes in creating IT support plans that work for each individual school and even facilitates financing and leasing assistance when needed. They are a customer-focused resource and view clients as partners. The company implements solutions that enhance information flow, increase student and data safety, and ultimately drive successful learning initiatives.

Julio began to develop his deep range of technological skills during an internship with Florida International University's Information Technology department. This rich experience turned into a full-time position that set him up for his next role with Ion Technologies, where he gained extensive on-the-job knowledge, holding such roles as field engineer, systems architect, systems integrator, and cabling infrastructure architect.

He attributes his overall success to his dedication to maintaining a strong work-life balance. Exercise has always been one of those key components. A lifelong athlete, Julio was a cornerback for the University of Central Florida football team. These days, he and his girlfriend, Manuela, along with their four children, incorporate physical activity into their routine, regularly working out and taking long walks together. They love to be outdoors and enjoy road trips – often to the beach.

Julio and his family live in Aventura, Florida, where they make it a point to sit down together for dinner every night. He says this is an important opportunity to reconnect after a long day.

To contact:
> IT for Education: A Division of Net A Corp
> Miami, Florida

- Email: jlopez@netacorp.com
- Web: https://www.itforedu.com
- Phone: 305-403-7582

CHAPTER 16

WILL YOU BE SUED IF YOUR DATA IS BREACHED?

BY TRENT MILLIRON
Founder & CEO – Kloud9 IT

WILL YOU BE SUED? YES, YOU PROBABLY WILL!

Large or small, long-established, or just launched, thousands and thousands of companies depend on IT systems to analyze customer data; to design, build and distribute intellectual property like games, software, or proprietary processes; to manage supply chains and manufacturing; to organize their human resource departments, and to conduct their financial affairs. As IT has become indispensable, the number of hackers and bad actors has multiplied, and both the frequency and the sophistication of their attacks have expanded dramatically.

Over the last decade, the rising tide of data breaches has exploded into the headlines. In today's litigious society, this means more lawsuits over lost or stolen data are sure to be filed.

Recent cyber security attacks and breakdowns at large companies have triggered class-action lawsuits, which resulted in payouts of many millions of dollars in settlements. The theft of credit card information from Home Depot's systems ended in a sizable settlement to account holders. A lawsuit over Target's 2013 personal information breach resulted in a payout of some $10 million to consumers and a whopping $39 million to banks. A new wave of litigation has risen since the 2021 Colonial Pipeline and Kaseya ransomware incidents, in part because so many downstream businesses were forced to temporarily shut down or severely restrict their IT processes.

As this chapter goes to press, T-Mobile has reported a massive theft of private information – social security numbers, dates of birth, phone, and PIN numbers – affecting 8 million current customers and possibly involving a total of some 40 million people, including former customers and credit applicants. There's no word yet on legal consequences.

The year 2019 saw some 337 confirmed ransomware events that also resulted in a data breach. That number doubled to 676 in 2020, with hacks and data exposures spanning the government, health care, retail, manufacturing, and technology sectors. As more and more companies experience crippling and costly data breaches, the number and sophistication of data breach lawsuits are also on the rise.

WHAT CAN TRIGGER DATA BREACH LAWSUITS?

When customer or personnel data files are breached, there is no shortage of advice for consumers who are worried about what to do. Tip list articles abound, along with more pointed advice on how to take legal action. The sources range from well-regarded consumer publications to law firms offering advice and consultations to wiki sites that cram tidbits of practical information between ad banners.

It's not uncommon for exposed individuals to sue the business that suffered the attack, sometimes by initiating class action suits and less often as individuals claiming compensation for damages due to negligence.

Often the MSP, as an IT contractor who recommends and installs tech tools, and manages security for clients, is next in line to be blamed – and sued – following a data breach. Breaches are costly; thus, businesses and their legal advisors look for another party to share the financial burden of stolen records as well as the costs of customer legal action. In some cases, a client could attempt to hold you legally accountable for conditions that allowed a breach in their own network.

HOW CAN YOU REDUCE THE RISK OF A DATA BREACH LAWSUIT?

Here are some things a small business can do to avoid a data breach lawsuit:

1) *Prevent the data breach altogether.* The best way to avoid legal action is to stop a data breach from ever happening. Work with your MSP to identify, install and maintain up-to-date end-point and firewall protections, encryption, and backup tools, and keep current on software patches, drivers, and updates.

2) *Reinforce the "human firewall."* With your consultant and your staff, create comprehensive cyber security training and staff policies that instill a culture of security and cybercrime prevention at every staff level, from the cubicles to the C-suite.

A RISK MANAGER SPEAKS

Recently I talked with Justin Reinmuth, Founder and CEO of the Technology Risk Underwriting Group. In business since 2004, TechRUG, as it's popularly known, manages technology risk for some 600 IT companies, covering broad categories such as cyber security, general liability, workers' compensation, employment practices, directors' and officers' coverage, and errors and omissions insurance.

I put the question at the heart of this chapter to Justin: Will you be sued if your data is breached? His response was surprising. "Many people will say yes," replied Justin. "I'd say, 'It depends.'" There are two factors to consider, he says. "Assuming that as an MSP or as a public-facing business you do have a contract with your client, what does your contract say you are and are not responsible for? Second, are you informing your clients that you use third-party vendors – for example, IT Glue or Office 365 – and that your company's acceptance of your vendors' terms and conditions includes end-user agreements that extend to your clients and customers as well? Your signature indicates that you accept your vendors' hold harmless and indemnification, and limitation of liability provisions, and so does your client's signature on a contract with your company. And, when assessing your eligibility for coverage, your risk manager might well ask to see your client's signature acknowledging this."

Justin goes on to say that a managed services agreement with the end client should commit the client to carry cyber liability insurance.

"It's well-known," says Justin, "that architects, lawyers, physicians, accountants – in short, professionals in many business categories – all these carry professional liability insurance policies," and when their businesses are IT-dependent, it's vital for them to add cyber insurance coverage.

LAYERS OF PROTECTION: INSURANCE PLUS CONTRACTS

Let's take a closer look at cyber liability insurance.

The Cybersecurity and Infrastructure Security Agency (CISA), a division of the US Department of Homeland Security, has as its mission to lead the national effort to understand and manage cyber and physical risk to our critical infrastructure. CISA defines cyber security insurance as coverage crafted to help mitigate losses from a variety of incidents – data breaches, business interruption, and network damage among them. The agency maintains that a robust cyber security insurance market could help reduce the number of successful cyber-attacks by (1) promoting the adoption of preventative measures in return for more coverage, and (2) encouraging the implementation of best practices by basing premiums on the insured's level of self-protection. However, many companies forego available coverage because of the perceived high cost of cyber security policies, confusion about what they cover, and uncertainty that their organizations will suffer a cyber-attack.

CISA is facilitating dialogue with leaders in academia, infrastructure owners and operators, insurers, chief information security officers (CISOs), chief security officers (CSOs), risk managers and others, in search of ways to expand the ability of the cyber security insurance market to address this emerging cyber-risk area. Discussion focuses on how a cyber-incident data repository could foster both the identification of emerging cyber security best practices and the development of new cyber security insurance policies that "reward" businesses for adopting and enforcing those best practices.

Besides targeted liability coverage, many large insurers offer their cyber policyholders access to tools and resources to manage and mitigate cyber-risk – both pre-breach as well as post-breach.

Today, both MSPs and their end clients need risk management protection more than ever because they face more risks – cyber security and data privacy challenges, plus compliance, technology, and vendor issues, plus increasing competition.

Like legal or medical malpractice insurance, professional liability insurance covers the MSP if a client alleges negligence in the performance of a contract; it protects the customer if a service provider is negligent.

First-party cyber liability insurance protects the end client's data from cyber liability risks, whatever the cause. It helps protect the end client and their customer in the event of data breaches and data losses that are not the fault of the MSP.

THE VITAL ROLE OF DETAILED CONTRACTS

As Justin Reinmuth says, just as your signature binds you to accept your vendors' hold harmless and indemnification, and limitation of liability provisions, your client's contract with your company should commit them to accept the same terms as you do.

Service contracts should include an insurance section that stipulates that the MSP will carry first-party cyber liability insurance and that the client also agrees to carry it.

A small business's contract with a client should also disclaim responsibility for hardware and software failures caused by third-party manufacturers and publishers.

Because data loss and compromise pose such a high risk for MSPs and clients, the service contract should also disclaim hardware and software failures related to backups and require customers to retain local backups of all critical data in addition to any backup services the MSP provides.

EVOLVING LEGAL PROTECTIONS FOR MSPs, THEIR CLIENTS, AND CONSUMERS

Some of us might long for a time before hacks and attacks became so common and so potentially devastating. But the old days of walk-in computer repair and seat-of-the-pants network management – the days before businesses and their customers became so dependent on privacy standards, system integrity, and reliability – are gone forever.

However, there are signs that new laws are taking into account the complex relationships of service providers, clients, and consumers in today's IT environment.

In Ohio, if you adhere to NIST, CMMC, HIPAA and a specified roster of other guidelines and standards, your MSP or consumer-facing business can be protected from liability because – as long as you both follow and document that you followed the standards – you are not automatically liable for losses due to a data breach. Utah has recently enacted a similar statute.

The comprehensive New York State SHIELD Act lays out clear definitions that protect the state's consumers and also defines the responsibilities of companies that collect and use private information. Rather than applying only to companies doing business in New York, the new law covers any person or business that owns or licenses private information of a New York resident. Even if your business is located outside New York, having New York-based customers can mean it applies to you. The definition of the term "private information" is expanded to include account numbers, biometrics, credit/debit card numbers, access codes, usernames, e-mail addresses, passwords, and security questions and answers. The definition of a "breach" now includes not just unauthorized acquisition but also unauthorized access of computerized data that compromises the security, confidentiality, or integrity of private information. It imposes new data security measures, requiring that companies adopt reasonable safeguards to protect the security, confidentiality, and integrity of private information. It also requires that an employee be designated to oversee cyber security operations.

To sum up, in today's attack-prone IT environment, it's realistic to assume that a security breach will occur and that sensitive data can be stolen, exposed, or exploited. Depending on the details, this could lead to lawsuits claiming that businesses serving consumers, as well as MSPs, are liable for resultant damage or losses.

These are some things we must do as managers of IT-intensive businesses. We must be rigorous about maintaining the highest security, backup, and update standards. We must be diligent in practice and meticulous in the documentation of our practices. Our service contracts and user agreements must describe the responsibilities of all parties in detail. Our customers and ourselves must carry cyber insurance policies that match our roles and responsibilities. If we incorporate all these precautions into daily practice – and can demonstrate strict compliance – we may be less likely to face litigation, and if we are sued, less likely to be judged negligent.

NOTE: Are you inspired to improve your company's contracts, cyber security, documentation, or risk management practices? Please take notice that the information presented here is meant for general informational purposes only and does not constitute formal advice on legal or risk management matters. You should contact your attorney for advice on contracts and legal liability and discuss the details of risk management and liability coverage with an insurance professional who specializes in cyber security.

About Trent

Trent Milliron is the founder and CEO of Kloud9 IT, a thriving managed services provider with offices in Columbus, Cleveland, and Akron, Ohio. Kloud9 IT has built a five-star reputation by offering a menu of services from day-to-day operating and maintenance support to IT security, to VOIP systems, to tailored cloud computing, for clients throughout the Cleveland, Akron, Canton, and Columbus metro areas.

Trent was born in Shelby, Ohio, the son of a steelworker and a homemaker. As a boy, he was obsessive about computers, reading computer magazines, visiting computer stores, and pestering his family to get a PC. Trent's wish came true when his father's job offered to help employees buy a computer for their families. Trent earned his BA in IT from Ohio University in 1999. Launching his career in the early dot-com era, he became keenly aware of the immense potential of IT, the value of strategic vision, and the pitfalls of poor planning.

When the dot-com bubble burst, Trent shifted to a role working with nonprofits in the Cleveland school system. He soon realized that many private and public entities don't truly understand IT and lack a clear idea of what to look for in IT service. This insight formed the basis for Kloud9 IT.

Trent founded Kloud9 IT in 2006 as a computer repair and consulting company aimed at helping businesses find tech solutions. Realizing that there was a broader customer base to serve and an expanding range of services to offer, he refashioned Kloud9 IT into a full-featured managed services provider. Trent refers to Kloud9's reasonable monthly rates as "Flat Fee IT."

Kloud9 IT employs the most talented technicians and engineers; the staff lives by the motto "Do it right the first time." Rather than "band-aid" an outdated, poorly performing network, the Kloud9 team builds from the ground up based on proven technology and best practices. The company employs both video and in-person training to bring the client's staff on board.

Kloud9 IT is a CMMC Registered Provider Organization providing security expertise for military and government contractors and others requiring high-level security standards. The company also delivers its own SOC-backed security services. Kloud9 specializes in IT services tailored to the legal, accounting, and title industries. The company is proud to offer Fortune 500–level IT services for a budget-friendly fixed monthly rate.

Trent researches extensively to stay abreast of innovations in technology and evolving security challenges. The company strongly supports the military and donates a portion of its annual profits to St. Jude Hospital, the Wounded Warriors Project, and local charities. In his leisure time, Trent enjoys golf and relaxing by the pool with family and friends. His bucket-list wish is to take flying lessons.

To contact Trent:

Trent Milliron, Founder & CEO, Kloud9 IT
- E-mail: tmilliron@kloud9it.com
- LinkedIn: https://www.linkedin.com/company/kloud9
- Twitter: https://twitter.com/kloud9it
- Facebook: https://www.facebook.com/Kloud9IT/
- Instagram: https://www.instagram.com/kloud9it/
- Blog: https://www.kloud9it.com/blog/
- Web: https://www.kloud9it.com/
- Phone: 1-844-KLOUD9IT (556-8394)

Kloud9 IT – Cleveland
9999 Granger Rd., Cleveland, OH 44125
Phone: 216-393-2484
Fax: 216-373-2323
https://www.kloud9it.com/locations/cleveland/

CPSIA information can be obtained
at www.ICGtesting.com
Printed in the USA
BVHW041035200422
634795BV00009B/200/J